MADE TO MARVEL

Made to Marvel: *Your Jaw Belongs on the Floor*

Copyright © 2021 by Travis Habbershon

All rights reserved.

ISBN: 9798715251596

A publication of Tall Pine Books

|| *talepinebooks.com*

*Printed in the United States of America

MADE TO MARVEL

YOUR JAW BELONGS ON THE FLOOR

TRAVIS HABBERSHON

This book is dedicated to my son, Haven Ryland Habbershon.

Haven, you have taught me so much, from your very first breath until now. Jesus has used you in so many ways to speak to me and help me. I've learned so much about our Heavenly Father by being your father. Being your Dad is one of the greatest things I'll ever do.

As your father, I write this book so that you will have something throughout your life that will continually help fan the flames of your faith in Christ. You will face many battles in life my beautiful son, my hope is that this Book (along with the Bible) will give you the courage to persevere through every trial and storm. These pages will help you keep your eyes on Jesus every step of the way. No matter what happens in your life–refuse to depart from Jesus.

Your Mom and I, read and prayed these Scriptures over you when you were first born.

This is your calling:

> Matthew 5:14-16 "You are the light of the world—like a city on a hilltop that cannot be hidden. No one lights a lamp and then puts it under a basket. Instead, a lamp is placed on a stand, where it gives light to everyone in the house. In the same way, let your good deeds shine out for all to see, so that everyone will praise your heavenly Father."

We love you, Haven!

—MOM AND DAD

ACKNOWLEDGMENTS

To my wife, Kelsey for all your love, encouragement and support, thank you for believing in me.

To my son, Haven, you continue to teach me so much, I'm so grateful I get to be your Dad, thank you little buddy!

To my mom, and my big sister, thanks for being my guardian angels my whole life. I love you!

To my Dad, I'm so proud of you and grateful Jesus gave us a real father and son relationship.

To the Shirk Family, for being the family with whom I first experienced the love of Jesus. I'm forever grateful for the seeds you planted in my young life.

To Nathaniel Tyler Mowery, thanks for helping me get clean and all the time you invested in me. You helped walk me through some of my deepest pain. I'm the man I am today because of you.

To Allan Scott, thanks for writing the forward and all the encouragement you gave me as you read through the manuscript.

To Matteah Fiske, Amanda Strauser, Aaron Crosson, Eddie Kepner, and the team at Tall Pine Books, thanks for helping bring this book to life. You've made the phrase, *"Team work makes the dream work!"* a beautiful reality.

To Pastor John and Joelle Walters, and my New Life Church family, thank you for giving me a place to learn and grow. Thank you for praying for me. Serving Jesus with you is one of the greatest joys of my life.

To Jesus, I love you. Thanks for bringing me out of the darkness and into your marvelous light. May You be glorified through this book. May it give people hope, break off chains, and put people's jaws back on the floor.

CONTENTS

Foreword   xi
Preface   xiii
Introduction   xvii

The Dream   I
1. Section 1: Devotion to Teaching   5
2. Section 2: Devotion to Fellowship   31
3. Section 3: Devotion to Communion   62
4. Section 4: Devotion to Prayer   85

Small Group Guide   109
About the Author   113

FOREWORD

It was about one o'clock in the afternoon when Travis and I had just sat down at a restaurant together. It was the first time that we had hung out one on one, and I was still getting to know this guy. I remember a waitress walking up to our table. Immediately, Travis asked this lady about a tattoo on her wrist. As that sparked conversation, our waitress began to share about a hard time she was going through. How she felt detached from God.

I watched Travis begin to tell this girl that Jesus loved her; that God had an amazing plan for her life. At one point, she almost couldn't speak. This waitress was so amazed that God would send someone to intersect her life in this way. She was blown away that God saw her and that He loved her. Fast forward a couple months, this encounter was life changing for this young lady. She began to go back to church and see God do things in her life that seemed impossible just a few months before.

I remember thinking as we left the restaurant, *"Who is this Travis guy?"* The whole thing left me amazed. I began to think, *"This is the life that Jesus has for every believer!"* My jaw was on the floor. It challenged my faith. It challenged *me*.

When I began to read this book I thought, *"Yup. The words that Travis wrote here match the content of his life."* Travis is fired up for Jesus. He's going as strong in year twelve as he was at the beginning of his relationship with the Lord. And it's important that you know that. He's smoking what he sells, and you can see the evidence of that in his life.

When I first met Jesus, I marveled everyday at what He was doing in and around me. Overtime, things began to feel different, less colorful. For those of us who have been walking with God for a while, life can get stale as we "go through the motions." But it doesn't have to! This book has encouraged me to get back to the basics. God doesn't make it complicated for His kids. If we want to feel like we felt in the beginning, we have to do the things we did in the beginning. Sometimes the *start* is where we *finish* the race.

And that's what this book is about. As believers in Jesus, we have been hardwired to see God do amazing things every day. Things that take our life from black and white into amazing three-dimensional technicolor. No matter whether you are new to Jesus, or have been following Him for many years, "Made to Marvel" will cause you to rethink your faith. It will inspire and challenge you. Encourage you and breathe fresh air into your walk with God. Your spirit will be refreshed, your belief stirred, and you will be in awe of what God begins to do in and through your life. Friends, every day your jaw belongs on the floor. **You weren't made for medi-ocre. You were made for more. You were Made to Marvel!**

—ALLAN SCOTT

PREFACE

"A deep sense of awe came over them all, and the apostles performed many miraculous signs and wonders." (Acts 2:43)

While pondering this verse, a question surfaced in my heart: *What makes up the awe factor?*

After a few seconds, the Lord gently whispered in my spirit, "Look at the previous verse!" I should have thought of that. The previous verse shows us four things to which the early believers were devoted:

"All the believers devoted themselves to the apostles' teaching, and to fellowship, and to sharing in meals (including the Lord's Supper), and to prayer." (verse 42)

They were *"all"* in *awe* because they were *"all"* devoted. *Awe* is to be the atmosphere of the church. Awe is amazement, but it's also deep reverence and respect for a holy God. I believe God is bringing His body back to a place of awe and wonder, just as it was when the church first started. He's resurrecting the fear of the Lord. The church needs more than smoke and lights. Fog machines and light shows don't break chains. Only the presence and power of God can do that.

The awe factor is birthed and sustained by a life of devotion to the teachings of Jesus, fellowship with other believers, times of communion and prayer. These four devotions make up the four sections of this book. In each section, I share a lot of Scripture, as well as my personal experience with each devotion. Then I provide practical examples and stories on how you can grow in each of these devotions in your life. This book is more than information, however. Through it, I believe you will receive an impartation of all the Lord has burned in my heart through my relationship with Him. A fresh flame is about to touch your heart.

Scripture reveals that *"a deep sense of awe came over them all."* The *"all"* is referring to the first three thousand people who came to believe in Jesus after the Holy Spirit was poured out and Peter preached his first sermon on the day of Pentecost. They lived in awe and wonder from the very beginning of their new life in Christ. Many begin in awe, but they don't stay in awe. God is ready to break off boredom and complacency in His body by giving us the gift of fresh hunger to know Him more.

There is more!

The enemy of growth in your relationship with Jesus is thinking you've arrived. Spiritual plateaus are dangerous. We must continue to allow the Lord to mold and shape us, no matter how long we've been following Him. That "been there/done that" mentality needs to die if your faith is going to thrive and survive in these days.

I can say with all honesty that since I truly surrendered my life to Jesus without reservation, I've lived in *awe* and *wonder*.

What saddens my heart are all the people I know for whom, when they describe their Christian lives, those two words are nowhere to be found. This is the reason I'm writing this book. I feel a call from God, a burden from the Lord, to help believers get back to the awesomeness of God. Reverence for the Lord needs to be restored. He is holy!

My hope is that through these pages your jaw will be back on the floor where it belongs, not just as you read this book but as you live every day following Jesus. Jesus enjoys blowing our minds. The best is yet to come. You were made to marvel!

A FEW THOUGHTS ON DEVOTION

True devotion has been lost. Check out this definition.

Devotion: *to adhere to **one**, constant to **one**, to give unremitting care to **a** thing, to persevere and not faint, to be in constant readiness for **one**.*

Devotion is what lovers do. Devotion isn't simply duty. If your devotion to the Lord is just religious duty, your life will be "doodie." Devotion is more than reading *Jesus Calling*, or some other devotional book, before you go to work in the morning. Having a morning devotion time doesn't make you a Christian, following and living in love with Jesus does. When you truly see how devoted God is to you, it changes you. You can't look at Jesus on the cross and stay the same. His *love* changes everything. When His love is seen and received, you reorient everything in your life so you can know your Rescuer and make your Rescuer known. Jesus is our Rescuer.

Ponder these questions…

- *Is Jesus the "One" you adhere to?*
- *Is Jesus the "One" you're constant to?*
- *Do you give unremitting care to your relationship with Him?*
- *Do your eyes stay fixed on Him in the storms of life?*
- *Do you live in constant readiness to talk to Him and hear from Him?*
- *Is Jesus your "One thing"?*

That's what it means to be devoted. When Jesus is your "One thing," it will change how you see everything. Your jaw will be where it belongs—on the floor—as you grow in intimacy and friendship with the Lord.

Here's a simple prayer to help you begin in this adventure:

Jesus, blow my mind with brand new discoveries of who You are. Forgive me of any complacency and soften my heart. Open my mind, precious Holy Spirit, to receive from You. Ignite me now with fresh fire and passion. In Jesus' name I pray. Amen!

INTRODUCTION

You were made to marvel. You were made to live a life of awe and wonder. If nobody ever told you that, I'm sorry. Life is more than bills, fears, addictions and anxieties. Life was never meant to be a grind. You were made to experience the glory of God. You were made to intimately know the One who made you. Your jaw belongs on the floor.

I can remember being a little kid and spending a lot of time under the Christmas tree, starring at the lights. I was fascinated by the brightness and the beauty of all the colors. The twinkling, the shimmering and all the shine made my heart feel alive. Worry and fear didn't seem to exist under the tree. Wonder has a way of washing away all worries and fears.

Another thing I loved was when my mom would drive us around our town to look at Christmas lights. We would drive around and check out all the decorated homes. There was one house that always went all out, similar to the Griswold's in the movie *National Lampoon's Christmas Vacation*. I could have starred at those lights forever. It was truly marvelous.

Somewhere along the line, as I got older, I started starring at the lights less. The things of this world grabbed my gaze. I had no anchor to Christ, so I was easily dragged away. Making friends and fitting in became more important. Paychecks and parties became the priority. Getting high and feeling good became my daily goal. I can look back now and see that the more I got my eyes off the lights, the darker my life became.

This landed me in full-blown drug addiction and isolation. I went from marveling at lights to hating my life. From smoking weed to smoking crack. From popping pills to shooting dope. From feeling "a part of" to feeling alone. Darkness became my norm. It seemed to swallow me up and I almost didn't make it out. I didn't know that I was made to marvel, not just as a kid but also as an adult.

Along with looking at the four devotions of the early church, and my journey with them, I'm excited and honored to share in these pages my personal story of how my jaw found its way back to the floor. This is my story, from *suicide* to *Savior*.

—Travis Habbershon

THE DREAM

I scheduled to release the title and cover of this book at the end of March 2021. Only a select few people knew the title and subtitle. On the morning of Tuesday March 16th, a friend and member of our church who had no idea the details of this book sent me a dream they had that night.

Here's the dream:

"I had a dream that you were speaking to a large group of people on a hilltop. The dream started at the end of your sermon and after you prayed, you said, "nobody is leaving until everybody stands where I am now and shares a scripture or a story of hope."

Immediately, everyone lined up on the stage steps, with a sense of eagerness to say something. Everyone started sharing and I ended up falling out of line twice. The first time I ran down to a nearby pavilion to grab my Bible. I booked it back up to the line.

The second time, I stepped out to help a girl who fell off the stairs onto a riser. A youth age boy stepped in to help. He started waving down a man who happened to be a youth pastor. This made me realize there were people on this hill top from a bunch of different churches in the area. Even though we go to different churches on Sunday, we are called to be the body of Christ. United and sharing about the Son of God TOGETHER. Helping one another.

So, the youth pastor said he would take care of her and told me to get back in line.

I ended up being the last person in line to stand at the microphone. I opened my Bible to Revelation and shared a scripture.

But after I was done speaking, I saw you, Travis Habbershon, sitting on the stage.

I came over to you because you were by yourself and had a look on your face as if you were thinking, **"Woah!" I mean, your jaw was dropped to the floor.**

I asked if you were okay and you said "Yeah, I'm just looking at all of God's Glory. Look at it." You pointed outwards.

So, I faced forward and looked into the distance.

At the beginning of my dream, the only light shining was the stage spotlight, it was pitch black everywhere else. But by the end of my dream, when I was looking out, the entire hilltop was engulfed in light and everyone on it cultivated light. On the hilltop, I seen a bunch of people praying with each other, so much hope, and revival taking place. Breakthrough was happening on this hill.

And even though the valley was still dark, it wasn't pitch black anymore. You could see, very faintly, everything going on in those depths. It was the most beautiful thing I have ever seen!"

* * *

WHEN MY FRIEND told me the dream… my jaw hit the floor. I began to tremble in the presence of God. Then in holy awe I shared with them what the title and subtitle of my book was… BOOM! their jaw hit the floor and they began praising Jesus. Plus, *Matthew 5:14-16* have been life verses to me since surrendering my life to Christ. Our God is Awesome! This book is a word from the Lord. You were made to marvel. Enjoy!

1

SECTION 1: DEVOTION TO TEACHING

"Nobody ever outgrows Scripture; the book widens and deepens with our years."—Charles Spurgeon

I've received many revelations, or what I like to call "light bulb moments," since growing in Christ, but perhaps one of the most profound was when I realized that most of what I had been taught about life, prior to beginning a relationship with Jesus, was a lie. Don't get me wrong, my mom did an amazing job raising me. She worked her butt off to keep a roof over our heads and food in our bellies. I just wasn't taught Jesus. Instead, I gravitated toward a lot of unhealthy influences. Jesus is life itself. If you're not taught Him, you live lost in a land of lies.

First John 1:2 says Jesus is the *One* who is life itself.

Here's the thing: when you're taught lies, you live a lie. I was lost in a lie until truth came into my life. Jesus is the way, the truth and the life. He's not just the way to the Father, some-day; He's the way to living the awestruck life *now*. To experience a life of awe and wonder, we need the right teaching from the right teacher.

The first component of the awe factor is a devotion to teaching. The Scripture says, *"All the believers devoted themselves to the apostles' teaching"* (Acts 2:42). What exactly was *"the apostles' teaching"*?

If we look at the apostle Peter's first sermon in Acts 2, we will discover the answer. After the Holy Spirit was poured out on 120 people in the upper room, the power of God drew the attention of many others. Peter then stood before the crowd of the *curious* and the *ridiculers* and prompted them to remember the predictions of the prophet Joel, because Joel's prophecy just kicked-off. Check this out:

> *"Then Peter stepped forward with the eleven other apostles and shouted to the crowd, "Listen carefully, all of you, fellow Jews and residents of Jerusalem! Make no mistake about this. These people are not drunk, as some of you are assuming. Nine o'clock in the morning is much too early for that. No, what you see was predicted long ago by the prophet Joel: 'In the last days,' God says, 'I will pour out my Spirit upon all people. Your sons and daughters will prophesy. Your young men will see visions, and your old men will dream dreams. In those days I will pour out my Spirit even on my servants—men and women alike—and they will prophesy. And I will cause wonders in the heavens above and signs on the earth below—blood and fire and clouds of smoke. The sun will become dark, and the moon will turn blood red before that great and glorious day of the Lord arrives. But everyone who calls on the name of the Lord will be saved."' (Acts 2:14–21)*

After explaining what was taking place and quoting Joel, Peter went right into dropping the J-Bomb! The J-Bomb is the name above every name—the name of Jesus. Look at the next verse:

*"People of Israel, listen! God publicly endorsed **Jesus the Nazarene** by doing powerful miracles, wonders, and signs through him, as you well know. (verse 22, emphasis added)"*

From Joel to Jesus.

What advice would we give Peter today? I think it would go something like this:

Now Peter, I know that you're excited about Jesus, and you just had fire on your head, but go slow when talking to people about Him. You don't want to offend anybody.

It was not the hour for passive Christianity *then* or *now*. The baptism of the Holy Spirt took Peter from a *passive people-pleaser* to a *passionate preacher*. He went from denying Jesus to unashamedly dropping the J-Bomb, and around three thousand lives were changed because of it. Peter didn't take long to drop the J-Bomb because it's the J-Bomb that blows up the enemy's plans. It's the J-Bomb that sets people free. It's Jesus that people *need.* Let's never forget that there is power in the name of Jesus. He is the teacher we need to teach people about.

Peter went from Joel to Jesus because Joel, along with every other Scripture in the Bible, points to Jesus.

"Jesus said it Himself: "The Scriptures point to me!" (John 5:39).

. . .

WHICH TAKES US TO THE PLAYGROUND...

While playing at a playground with my son, Haven, I heard the words "Jesus Christ" coming out of a father's mouth as he ranted and argued on his cell phone. In his anger and frustration, he said "J.C." a few times—and he wasn't praising the Lord. He was speaking loudly on the phone and there were a lot of kids around. One grandma standing close to me looked annoyed and offended by what she heard.

I immediately began to pray and ask God for some words to share with the man. While communing with Jesus and watching my son play, Haven took off running to another area of the playground—right beside the bench where this guy was sitting. God has a way of helping me move into action.

I followed my son, reached out my hand to the man, and said, "How's it going, bro? My name is Travis." The man shook my hand and replied, "I am having one of those days." I said, "The name you were saying is the solution to your problems," to which the man replied, "What name?" "Jesus Christ!" I told him.

Drop the J-Bomb!

This started an amazing, God-ordained conversation. This man was hurting and had some things fall through that he had really been hoping for. After talking to him for a minute, I understood his frustration. At one time in my life, I probably would have been offended at this man's actions and by the language he used at a children's playground, but now, I had empathy in my heart. When I gave my life to Jesus, He gave me a new heart and a new spirit.

"And I will give you a new heart, and I will put a new spirit

in you. I will take out your stony, stubborn heart and give
you a tender, responsive heart." (Ezekiel 36:26)

I honestly didn't even hear anger and frustration; I heard a cry for help. This man didn't need to be reprimanded; he needed love—and love lives in me, and His name is Jesus. No one really wants to be swearing up a storm around kids at a playground. This man was lost.

Don't forget, Romans 2:4 (NKJV) says,

"The goodness of God leads you to repentance."

This man needed Jesus and a reminder of God's goodness. He was saying the right name but with the wrong heart. A listening ear goes a long way when witnessing to others.

We talked for a while and watched our kids play together. Just by talking about Jesus and shining His light, this man's whole countenance and demeaner changed in a few minutes. I shared the goodness of God with him and the freedom that Jesus has made possible in my own life. I gave him my phone number and we prayed. I love church in the park.

If I would have taught him something other than Jesus, such as an expression of offense and frustration or "How dare you talk like that around my kid!" (me, me, me etc.), we never would have had the chance to watch our kids play together, and we never would have had a chance to pray together.

Sure, I could have talked about anger management, and perhaps that would have been helpful, but I'd rather share about the One who removes stony, stubborn hearts. Jesus doesn't just help us, He also transforms us from the inside out. You can be a new creation in Christ. Old things really do pass away—including anger—and all things really do become new—including you! Only Jesus can do that.

That's why it's important to talk and teach about Him. Drop the J-Bomb! Blow up the enemy's plans! Talk about Joel, but just make sure you get to Jesus. He is the ultimate treasure.

TREASURE CHEST

Many homes in America have a treasure chest that is never opened. This unopened treasure chest has left many people spiritually dead and empty. Television and video games have taken priority over this treasure. Cell phones and constant scrolling have made thousands of hearts grow cold to its warmth. Constant busyness has blinded many minds to its worth. So many people have money and material possessions, but they remain spiritually broke. Many others have a surface smile but no internal joy.

Meanwhile, this treasure chest sits on a shelf, coated with dust. But here's some good news about this treasure chest: even dust cannot hinder its value. Even with dust, the chest remains a precious treasure, waiting to be opened and discovered.

What is sad is that this treasure chest doesn't even have a lock. It can be opened and enjoyed at any time. There's life in this treasure chest, yet many people settle for a lifeless existence.

Families have split because the chest was never opened. Addictions have started because the chest was never opened. Resentment has grown because the chest was never opened. Divorce has taken place because the chest was never opened. Hatred has remained because the chest was never opened.

People are in prison because the chest was never opened. People are dead because the chest was never opened. Chains remain because the chest is never opened. Confusion remains because the chest is never opened. Racism remains because the chest in never opened. Sin remains because the chest is never opened. Wonder has been washed away because the chest was never opened.

The most purchased treasure chest of all time has become the most unopened and neglected treasure chest of all time. Those who neglect this treasure never live triumphant lives. Their true purpose and identity remain lost as they settle for a spiritually depleted life.

Oh yeah, in case you are still wondering, the treasure chest I'm talking about is *the Bible*. God's Word is treasure, but only to those who love God and know that they desperately need Him.

My hope is that every Christian would rediscover this great treasure and knock the dust off their Bibles. You won't have much of a witness without it. You won't discover all that's in it if you don't open it. A Bible isn't something you keep around your home to look "spiritual"; it's daily bread that revitalizes the soul and helps you grow in the knowledge of God. Looking spiritual and becoming spiritual are two different things. Those who are truly spiritual have God's Word as the main source of their daily diet.

You don't have to stay broken, bound or bored. Open the chest!

> *"I rejoice in your word like one who discovers a great treasure." (Psalm 119:162)*

When you encounter Jesus through His Word, the Bible, and you see that it is alive and more than ink on paper, building devotion to it won't be a problem.

This, of course, requires that you open the book.

Another revelation that came into my mind when I initially began to see God move in my life and draw me to Himself was this: *I've never read the Bible. I've heard a lot of people talk about the Bible, but I've never opened it myself.*

This God-given lightbulb moment opened the door for Him to speak to me in a real, personal way. This was the birthing ground for my devotion to His teaching, and for the those He appointed to teach me. This is how I became a passionate lover of Jesus with a hunger for His Word.

Little did I know that my lightbulb moment would come from the darkest day of my life. This encounter you are about to read is why I'm a Christian; *this* got me looking at the Light again.

THE BIG REVEAL

As I clocked into work that morning, I knew it was going to be my last day—not just at work but on this earth. The year was 2007. At that time, I had been trapped in the prison of drug addiction for many years, and the only solution I could come up with was to kill myself. I had lost all hope. I hated myself, and when you hate yourself, suicide seems normal. The thought of ending my life consumed me, day in and day out.

I started work at 7 that morning, and by 9:30, I was walking out the door. I told my supervisors, "I'm leaving." They thought I was talking about leaving work, but I was ready to leave this earth. Dying was the only thought on my mind. I walked to my apartment in the darkest tunnel vision of my life with the words, *Kill yourself, kill yourself, kill yourself,* running through my head. It was like I was already dead.

When I entered my apartment, I grabbed a bottle of 50–60 pills, put them all in my mouth and chugged some water. Then I laid on my couch in my work clothes, hoping to die. I didn't call anybody; I didn't write a note; I just wanted to be dead and gone. I believed that everyone would be better off without me.

Let me just stop for a moment and say, if you are having suicidal thoughts, those thoughts are lies. I know things are tough right now, but there is hope. The very fact that you're reading these words right now is a sign that God is trying to get your attention. He put this book in your hands because He loves you. He's not finished with you and He hasn't given up on you. You are not alone. You are not unloved. You are not a failure.

Take a moment and pray this simple prayer: "Heavenly Father, take away these lies and fill me with your truth, right now! In Jesus' name I pray. Amen!

KNOCK, KNOCK

After swallowing those pills, *one* hour went by…then *four* hours… then *eight* hours…then *sixteen* hours…then *twenty-four* hours…then *thirty hours.* And still, I was out cold on my couch.

Then, *thirty-two* hours after I swallowed those pills, I miraculously heard a knock on my door.

My whole body was covered in a bright-red rash and the left side of my body was completely numb. My pants were soaked with urine and my mind was full of confusion. I had never been in a more delirious state in my life. I opened the door and saw a friend of mine. Immediately, he knew something was seriously wrong with me. I didn't know what day it was. I thought I was late for work. I was talking crazy.

I tried to leave for work, but my friend said, "Dude, its five in the evening, not five in the morning. What's wrong with you?"

I thought it was 5 a.m. and that he was lying to me, so I made him walk me to a payphone down the street so I could call work. As we walked, I remember seeing a kid riding a bike. It never dawned on me that kids don't ride bikes that early in the morning. When we got to the payphone, I called my work and they said, "Travis, you left early yesterday and missed this whole day."

I had taken those pills around 10 a.m. the day prior. It was now 5 p.m. the next day. I had been unconscious for thirty-two hours when I heard my friend's knock.

After I got off the payphone, my friend went his way and I went mine. My friend went to a bar and told some people about my condition. Some family friends happened to be sitting a couple of barstools away. They overheard what my friend was saying and reached out to my sister, who got ahold of my mom.

My family intervened, and a week later, I was getting help in rehab.

That is how grace works. I wanted to die, but instead, I got help. I tried to check out, but instead, God checked in. Grace is undeserved favor—a gift from God, an expression of His love that empowers us to change.

This was the first of two rehabs. Even though I struggled to get clean for a while, I knew in my heart that there was something significant in that knocking. After I became clean and started searching for God, I had the realization that I had never opened a Bible before, as well as the revelation that I needed to.

So, I did. I randomly opened it and landed in the book of Revelation. I didn't know there were sixty-six books in the Bible. I just flipped it open in faith with the hope that I would land on something that could help me in my search. I started reading. Nothing really made sense to me, but I kept reading.

Then, by divine appointment, I got to these life-changing, God-revealing, awe-inspiring words from Jesus:

> *"Look! I stand at the door and knock. If you hear my voice and open the door, I will come in, and we will share a meal together as friends." (Revelation 3:20)*

I couldn't believe what I was reading. I was awestruck as the presence of God came into my little apartment. It was like Ty Pennington from the TV show *Extreme Makeover: Home Edition* just shouted, "Move that bus!"—and on the other side of the bus stood my smiling Savior. This was my "big reveal." Then, the still small voice of my King whispered to my heart, "It was Me, Travis. I knocked on your door. I work through people. Will you let Me in? I want to be your Friend."

In that moment, everything changed. A veil was removed. Blinders fell away.

Jesus spoke and revealed Himself to me because He loves me. I've been devoted to His teaching and His touch ever since. My jaw hit the floor, and ever since that day, I've lived in awe and wonder. This is not a hype statement; it's true.

Jesus knocked on my door that day. He sent my friend because He wanted to be my Friend. He had a plan and purpose for my life beyond my wildest dreams. Jesus did for me what I couldn't do for myself. He loved me back to life. On my darkest day, He came for me and refused to let the grave take me. Without Him, I'm not here. I'm only able to write this book because He rescued me. All glory to King Jesus!

This verse says it all:

> *"Unless the Lord had helped me, I would soon have settled in the silence of the grave." (Psalm 94:17)*

Something died during those thirty-two hours. What died was the lie that I could do life on my own. I had to stop being my own teacher. Here's something else that will stir up awe and wonder: I was unconscious for *thirty-two hours* and Jesus spoke to me through *Revelation 3:20*. That's cool!

For all I know, I did die, but Jesus came and breathed the breath of life back into me. He still resurrects dead and addicted lives. His Word, the Bible, is alive!

So, open the Bible and you'll hear His sweet voice. God's Word is a treasure chest. After you hear Him once, you'll want to hear Him again.

I read His Word every day, and every day, I let His Word read me. I cherish my time in the Word; I love His voice. I welcome the *encouragement* and the *correction* it brings.

If your Bible has dust on it, then dusty or dry probably describes your life. Let this verse become your heart's cry: *"I lie in the dust; revive me by your word"* (Psalm 119:25).

It is crucial, my friends, that you develop a "Word-Walk Life."

> Psalm 119:133 says, "Guide my steps by you word, so I will not be overcome by evil."

When you have a Word-Walk Life—a life guided by the Word of God—you will live a victorious life. Evil, temptation, fear and sin cannot overcome you when you are guided by His voice. When you are guided by God's voice, you will not be overcome by evil; you'll be an overcomer.

Here are four simple keys to help you establish a Word-Walk Life:

1. Read the Word
2. Ponder the Word
3. Pray the Word
4. Declare the Word

It's time to knock the dust from your Bible and become a walking revival. It's time to get back to church, come under the teaching of God's Word and live a life of awe and wonder. You were made to marvel.

DID YOU CATCH THAT?

> "How amazing are the deeds of the Lord! All who delight in him should ponder them. Everything he does reveals his glory and majesty. His righteousness never fails." (Psalm 111:2–3)

Did you catch that? This is a question often asked when two people are having a conversation and one of them wants to make sure the other person understands what they are trying to say.

If you *catch it*, it means you didn't *miss it.*

That is why pondering Scripture is such an important practice. Pondering is the pathway to receiving revelation. Pondering is the opposite of hurrying. We must ponder His ways and His words.

Pondering allows truth to be trapped (caught) in our minds so that internal transformation can occur. Nothing changes if His words and ways go in one ear and out the other. Only trapped truth renews the mind. Only trapped truth transforms.

This is Romans 12:2 in action:

> *"Don't copy the behavior and customs of this world, but let God transform you into a new person by changing the way you think. Then you will learn to know God's will for you, which is good and pleasing and perfect."*

Our minds change when we intentionally ponder His words and ways. It's time to slow down and simmer in His presence, that we might ponder Jesus and all His ways so we can catch everything He wants to teach us.

The Bible isn't merely to be read; it's also to be chewed, consumed, taken in and pondered. When you chew it, you'll be changed by it! When you read it, and let it read you, you'll reveal Jesus to the world around you. Jesus doesn't want you to miss what He's speaking to you; He's wants you to "catch" the fact that He directs you in His Word so that you will take time and ponder it.

Everything He does *reveals* His glory. This includes the work He does in YOU! You are called to reveal His glory.

Along with digging into the treasure chest of Scripture, Jesus has used my relationship with my son, Haven, in incredible ways to teach me and speak to me. Children truly are a gift from God. Haven has always been a powerful frequency that God uses to speak to me. I've learned a lot about the Father by being a father.

"I'M SEEING YOU DAD"

To allow for Jesus to reveal His glory to me through the Scriptures, I must take my eyes off other things. Something must be closed for something new to be opened. I love how Psalm 119:37 says it: *"Turn my eyes from worthless things, and give me life through your word."*

I believe this is a prayer, but I also believe love is the only answer to this prayer. Love for Jesus will keep your eyes fixed on Him, and off of worthless things. Devotion grows out of love.

One time, when Haven was three years old, he was facing me, lying on his bed in an awkward position after I put a movie on his TV.

I asked him, "Haven! Why are you lying like that? You can't see the TV."

He responded, "I'm seeing you, Dad!"

My heart began to melt in this father-and-son moment. "I'm seeing you, Dad!" As his words sunk deeper into my heart,

God began to whisper to me, "In the same way you cherish moments like this with your son, I too cherish moments like this with you, My son."

When we turn our eyes away from worthless things and give our attention to Jesus, when we look at Him, it pleases Him. Haven turned from the TV to see me. He took his attention off the movie and gave it to me. "I'm seeing you, Dad!" are words every father cherishes, including our heavenly Father. Haven was looking at me because he loves me, and, likewise, we will gladly look at Jesus when we love Him. When we love Him, we will treasure His words and find *life* through them.

Worthless things drain us, but His Word refreshes and revives us.

"HOLD ME, DAD!"

Another time, while sitting with my son on the couch watching *Curious George*, Haven drew closer to me and said, "Hold me, Dad. Hold me, Dad!" Being on the same couch with my son and holding him are two different things.

Haven was basically saying, "Dad, we're close, but I want to be closer."

Our heavenly Father desires this kind of closeness with His kids. Jesus doesn't just want to sit on a couch with you; He wants to hold you. He doesn't just want to hold you one day a week while sitting in a pew; He wants to be close to you each and every day. He wants to father us because He loves us. As Haven drew near to me on the couch that day, I drew near and snuggled him as we watched the curious life of Curious George.

Check out this promise:

"Come close to God, and God will come close to you."(James 4:8)

The teaching that comes from being held is priceless. Jesus doesn't just want to teach us through His words, He also wants to teach us through His touch, His presence. He communicates a lot by holding us. Yes, we need His words, but we also need to be held.

I've learned a lot about God's heart by being held in God's arms. Busyness robs us of the experience of being held by God. Busyness is the thief of intimacy with the Lord. It's important to prioritize time with the Lord. We make dates and appointments for everything else—doctors, dentists, family, friends, etc.—*why not Jesus?* Jesus, the One who is life itself, would never give you a schedule that cuts Him out of your life.

If you don't have time for Him, *who is in charge?*

(Stop! Don't just bypass this question without honest reflection)

If you're in charge, you are in danger. It is in God's presence that we receive His direction for our lives. If you're not being held by Him, you're probably not hearing from Him either. If you remain in charge, your faith will flatline. When I tried to run the show in my life, it didn't turn out too well. Only a fool would refuse to be held. If Jesus is *Lord*, He won't be *last*. If He's last on your list, He's not Lord of your life.

My son is usually running around at 90 mph, bouncing from here to there, so I cherish the moments when he says, "Hold me, Dad!" Jesus wants to hear those same three words from you. He's watching and waiting for us to stop, put down our to-do list, and cry out, "Hold me, Dad!" If this becomes your prayer, I promise, you will learn a lot.

Life is found through His words, but also through His touch. His words draw us into His arms.

WHAT JESUS SAYS ABOUT HIS TEACHING

Jesus closes out the Sermon on the Mount with a power illustration:

"Anyone who listens to my teaching and follows it is wise, like a person who builds a house on solid rock. Though the rain comes in torrents and the floodwaters rise and the winds beat against that house, it won't collapse because it is built on bedrock. But anyone who hears my teaching and doesn't obey it is foolish, like a person who builds a house on sand. When the rains and floods come and the winds beat against that house, it will collapse with a mighty crash." (Matthew 7:24–27)

Does "mighty crash" describe your life right now?

If you answered "Yes" to that question, It's time for a new teacher. Jesus clearly states in this passage that a life built on Him is built on solid rock. You might get wet from the rain, and a little windburned from time to time, but your days of crashing are over when Jesus becomes your teacher. Mighty crash no longer describes your life. Build on the bedrock and remain standing. We build on the bedrock by being a doer of the word and not a hearer only. We first *listen* and then we *follow* the direction of the teaching by taking the appropriate action. *Hearing* without *doing* is not *wise*.

. . .

"But don't just listen to God's word. You must do what it says. Otherwise, you are only fooling yourselves." (James 1:22)

Doers of the word become unshakeable in the world. I've been through many storms since getting clean and sober, but because my life is built on the Rock and I continually cling to Jesus in child-like dependence, I have not had to get high or drunk to get through them.

UNSHAKEABLE

A Christian brother of mine was having invasive surgery for stomach cancer. One day, while he was still in the hospital recovering from the surgery, I called to offer some words of encouragement. He answered the phone, and in a scary tone, he said, "This...is...Fred's ghost," all while trying to hold back his laughter.

This guy almost died, but now he was laughing and having fun. I had called to encourage him, but guess what? He ended up encouraging me! The next thing I knew, he was telling me about how he had been ministering to the person in the bed beside him, and then he began giving me different Proverbs to read. Naturally, I was shocked.

I was amazed as I got off the phone that day. I expected my friend to be down and out, depressed, but it was like his cancer and the surgery didn't faze him or his faith at all. I'd seen other people go through cancer and the surgeries associated with it who were bitter and blaming God through the whole process. They asked questions like, "Why me, God?"

This was different. This was solid faith in Jesus. This was a house built on solid rock—and I wanted it. I wanted a faith that is unshakeable. The rain came for my friend, but it didn't change him. Now, several years later, he's cancer-free and still on fire for Jesus. Sickness never fazed the fire of his faith.

Here's a thought: *Why was I shocked? Why do testimonies like this shock us?*

For me, it was because I had rarely seen faith like that in action. I'd seen a lot of people crumble and give up during the storms in life, but now, I had witnessed a house built on the solid rock, Jesus Christ.

Brothers and sisters, this should be normal, and it will be normal when Jesus is your teacher. I thank God for my friend, who showed me what faith looks like in the face of a storm. This isn't a result of mustering up faith in the moment of a trial; this is the fruit of a life of devotion to Jesus and His teaching prior to the rain falling.

My friend lived out this verse:

> *"The godly offer good counsel; they teach right from wrong. They have made God's law their own, so they will never slip from his path." (Psalm 37:30–31)*

Question: *Are you tired of crashing, relapsing, slipping and back-sliding? Are you tired of being lukewarm?*

If God's law doesn't become your own, you're in trouble. Here's the good news: if God's Word makes its home in your heart and becomes personal to you, you won't have to keep crashing. It is possible to live a faithful life. It is possible to stay on God's path, no matter what!

Listen to me closely, you don't ever have to get high again, watch porn again, cheat on your spouse again or live in a way that's not God's best for you—ever again. You can be free, you can live by faith, you can build your life on the solid rock and live unshakably.

PAY ATTENTION

I was sitting on the couch putting on my shoes one morning as Haven was coming down the stairs singing. We love a good tune in the morning at the Habbershon's, don't you? There's nothing like getting ready for the day while being serenaded by your son.

Well, until this happened...

One moment, Haven was singing; the next moment, I heard him tumbling down the stairs, crashing at the bottom and crying. From singing to crying in a moment, all by not paying attention.

> Proverbs 4:26 says, "Give careful thought to the paths for your feet and be steadfast in all your ways" (NIV).

A key to being steadfast and firm in all your ways is taking time and giving "careful thought" prior to making decisions in life. When you "give careful thought," you'll "be steadfast in all your ways." Careful thought is the pathway to becoming steadfast. When you're steadfast, you're ready, you're prepared, you're established, you're stable and you're secure.

This proverb, when applied, will...

1. Help you to break free from impulsive living and decision making
2. Help you to spot the enemy's schemes in your life
3. Strengthen your relationship with God

4. Help you to grow in your awareness of God and His presence in your daily life

It is in the place of *"careful thought"* that we can hear from Jesus, connect to His heart and His power, and seek His guidance. *"Careful thought"* is a spiritual antenna through which the Holy Spirit communicates to us. Without this antenna, communication is hindered. When you give *careful thought*, you are giving God your attention and receiving His divine direction. That's why it's important to have a *quiet time* to pray about your day before it begins.

The minute you stop giving *"careful thought"* is the minute you start falling down. The enemy waits for believers to drop their spiritual antennae, and then he attacks.

I've seen people go from *living-clean* to *using* drugs again because they stopped paying attention. I've seen people go from *sober* to being a *slobbering drunk* again because they stopped paying attention. I've seen people go from *married* to *divorced* because they stopped paying attention. I've seen people go from *alive* to *dead* because they stopped paying attention.

Vigilance is important. When you're vigilant, you're alert and watchful, not paranoid and fearful. God wants to grow our awareness of Him and of approaching danger.

> *"Stay alert! Watch out for your great enemy, the devil. He prowls around like a roaring lion, looking for someone to devour." (1 Peter 5:8)*

As a dad, I've noticed my two most repeated phrases to my son are, "Haven, I love you" and "Haven, pay attention!" God repeats both, a lot, throughout His Word. So, I guess I'm just a chip off the old block.

Giving careful thought to his Word, meditating and chewing on it, means devoting your time to understanding it. It's easy to get distracted by things in life to the point that you're not paying attention anymore. The enemy loves it when we lose focus on what matters most. Satan is the one who is behind distraction. Staying devoted to prayer and the Word will keep you from falling into the trap of distraction. You don't have to keep falling down the stairs.

DEVOTION OVER DISTRACTION

If you want to remain devoted to Jesus' teaching, you must become a bird that doesn't budge.

Looking out the window at our backyard bird feeder, my wife, Kelsey, said, "Look at all those birds." I looked and saw about twenty birds storming our feeder. As I watched them chow down, the noise of a vehicle coming down the alleyway startled them and they all flew away in fear, except for *one* bird that did not budge. It continued to dine on the food in the feeder. As I watched the one bird that remained and continue to feast, a thought came to me: *The other birds are missing out.*

They missed out on a feast because of a noise. I continued to ponder this, and the Holy Spirit began to teach me. Noises, or distractions, are the enemy's main tactics to stop us from feeding on the Word of God and spending time in prayer. I want to be a bird that doesn't budge when I open my Bible. I want to be a bird that doesn't budge when I pray and worship the Lord. If the enemy can budge you, he will continue to thump you. But if you become unbudgeable in the Bible and in the place of prayer, there is nothing hell can do to stop you from experiencing spiritual growth, developing Christ-like character and deepening your intimacy with the Lord.

Jesus said, *"People do not live by bread alone, but by every word that comes from the mouth of God"* (Matthew 4:4).

The enemy knows this. That's why he works overtime trying to disconnect you from your life source by sending a million distractions. If you don't feed your spirit, you'll face a spiritual death. If you don't pray, your faith will slowly decay.

Birds that don't budge are filled and continue to grow, but birds that fly away at the slightest noise, thought, fear or to-do list simply don't.

I believe that Mary of Bethany is one of the greatest biblical examples of a bird that doesn't budge.

> *"As Jesus and the disciples continued on their way to Jerusalem, they came to a certain village where a woman named Martha welcomed him into her home. Her sister, Mary, sat at the Lord's feet, listening to what he taught. But Martha was distracted by the big dinner she was preparing. She came to Jesus and said, "Lord, doesn't it seem unfair to you that my sister just sits here while I do all the work? Tell her to come and help me." But the Lord said to her, "My dear Martha, you are worried and upset over all these details! There is only one thing worth being concerned about. Mary has discovered it, and it will not be taken away from her." (Luke 10:38–42)*

Martha was distracted; Mary was devoted. Mary was awestruck. These distractions robbed Martha from the only thing worth being concerned about—sitting at Jesus' feet, learning from Him. This is the foundation of the awestruck life. Mary knew she was made to marvel.

Have you invited Jesus in, but shut Him out with busyness? Inviting someone into your home and never talking to them would be considered rude and inconsiderate. Jesus wants to talk with you and teach you. Without hearing His voice, He can't be Lord of your life. Without hearing His voice, you can't be led by Him.

If your jaw hasn't been on the floor, maybe this is the reason.

Serving without *sitting* leads to burnout. *Doing* without *dining* leads to depletion. Both are needed but one is needed *first.* Mary discovered the greatest treasure, *have you?*

When distractions end, wonder begins.

When you stop letting distractions rob you, you'll see the wonders of His love all around, and you won't miss them when they're right in front of you.

REMAIN A STUDENT

> *"Students are not greater than their teacher. But the student who is fully trained will become like the teacher." (Luke 6:40)*

No matter where we are in our journey with Jesus, we can always make a fresh commitment to His leadership in our lives. The early believers were devoted to learning about Jesus. They remained students.

Bible studies are still important. Small groups are still important. Sunday services are still important. Asking questions is still important. Time alone with Jesus with an open Bible and heart is still important.

Allowing God to teach you opens opportunities to intervene with love and truth in the lives of someone who needs it. With a knock on the door, God can bring transformation to your life. His knocking reveals our need for Him, but also His desire to be with us. Disciples dine! Through the Word—the ultimate treasure—you learn to be steadfast, bold and on fire for Him. When you learn who God is, there is no room for depression, addiction or fear in your life. When God knocks at the door, it is because He has something to teach you, something that will change your life. It's your job to make sure you answer His knock.

Remain a student and you will remain in awe. Remain teachable and you'll experience continued transformation and growth. Your jaw belongs on the floor!

2

SECTION 2: DEVOTION TO FELLOWSHIP

"I am looking for the fellowship of the burning heart—for men and women of all generations everywhere who love the Savior until adoration becomes the music of their soul until they don't have to be fooled with and entertained and amused. Jesus Christ is everything, all-in-all."
—A. W. Tozer

Alone, we fall, but together, we stand. Alone, we face defeat, but together, we succeed. Devotion to fellowship is the second component of the awe factor. Devotion to fellowship is paramount in completing the mission Jesus gave us and to living the jaw-dropping Christian life.

I wouldn't be where I am today without friends. Without the strength that comes through friendship, I never would've found my way out of the dark. Since getting clean and sober, friendship and fellowship have been one of the greatest blessings in my new life in Christ. Many friends have been there for me over the years. Many have answered the phone in times of struggle and pain. Many have prayed for me. Many have hugged me and told me I could make it. I have found "the fellowship of the burning heart" that Tozer wrote about. This is a warmth you don't want to miss. The fellowship of the burning heart is born when brothers and sisters in Christ get the same heart tattoo.

HEART TATTOO

I believe the disciples probably forgot many things Jesus taught them in their time together before He went to the cross (over three years of teachings!). But I also believe there were some things Jesus told them that they never forgot, things that became immediately tattooed on their hearts by the Holy Spirt as He spoke them.

Here's one:

> *"I no longer call you slaves, because a master doesn't confide in his slaves. Now you are my friends, since I have told you everything the Father told me." (John 15:15)*

When Jesus says, *"Now you are my friends,"* it changes your life; it marks you. He was revealing to His disciples that His teaching and training wasn't just about duty and religion, but about growing in intimacy and relationship with Him. In the process of becoming their friend by laying down His life for them, Jesus said, *"Now you are my friends."* This teaches us that friendship comes through sharing and confiding in one another. God wants to share with you!

When I opened the Bible to the book of Revelation, Jesus said to me, "It was Me who knocked on your door. I work through people. Will you let me in? I want to be your friend." It was then I felt an indescribable love that has forever changed me.

Here's a jaw-dropping statement that never gets old: I'm friends with Jesus! Wow! Ponder that. Let the Holy Spirit tattoo that on your heart. This heart tattoo continues to keep me burning with the love of God, and it has also served as an anchor that has held me through many storms. From time to time, the enemy comes with his lies in an attempt to convince me that Jesus is not my friend, but when you've been tattooed, branded and marked as a friend of Jesus, you carry that truth as a constant reminder. This is a heart tattoo you can't afford to live without.

When you come together with others who have received the same heart tattoo—the revelation of friendship with Jesus that you receive by spending time with Him—you'll find yourself in the fellowship of the burning heart. The fellowship of the burning heart is born when friends and lovers of Jesus are connected and become friends, one to another.

The fellowship of the burning heart is a place where hearts can't remain cold. Chains break there. Depression is destroyed there. Lies are removed there. Everyone needs this heart tattoo. It's my personal favorite. You get it by spending time with Jesus.

When Mary sat at Jesus' feet and learned from Him in Luke 10:38-42, I believe she was receiving this heart tattoo. Jesus didn't send Mary off to serve with Martha because He wasn't done teaching truth and tattooing her heart. Martha missed becoming a friend of Jesus in that moment because of her misplaced priorities. Reader, don't let this happen to you. Jesus doesn't merely want you to serve Him; He wants your heart. He wants to be your friend.

Because friendship matters to God, friendship should also matter to us. People pursue a lot of things in life that don't really matter. Fame doesn't matter, *friendship matters*. Fortune doesn't matter, *friendship matters*.

Jesus also said,

> *"There is no greater love than to lay down one's life for one's friends."* (John 15:13)

I want to give you permission to get this tattoo. You won't regret it, and others will benefit because of it. Now, it's time to slay the giant that is keeping many from experiencing the joy and freedom of this most holy heart tattoo.

BEWARE THE NEW DRUG

Pay attention to what I'm about to say: human connection is more important than internet connection! If you panic more when you lose internet connection than you do when you lose a friend, something is wrong. It's time to wake up! If you are sadder when your phone dies than when a friendship dies, something is seriously wrong.

In our disconnected world, we are being destroyed. We've become numb to our need for each other. We've lost our devotion to each other.

Connecting through a screen isn't enough. Screens are keeping many from experiencing the fellowship of the burning heart. Screens have destroyed real intimacy.

Satan has unleashed a new drug that is destroying more families than heroin and cocaine combined. It's called "the screen." It is subtle in its attack, and because everyone has one, it doesn't seem like that big of a deal.

Please, please, please...*hear me!*

People living together and not even *knowing* each other is a big deal. Going through a day without making eye contact with someone is a big deal.

The family dinner table has been robbed, and most people are blind to it. Kids are becoming addicted to pornography at ridiculously young ages. Cyberbullying has caused many of our youth to kill themselves. Marriages are being destroyed through chat rooms. If you're still sleeping, it's time to wake up. We are losing a generation.

A question for you to seriously ponder: If someone needs a helping hand, would you drop your phone?

I don't know about you, but I would rather hold a *hand* than a *phone*. I would rather have eye contact than screen time. A text is nice, but a hug is better. Likes are cool, but *agape love* is better. Followers are fine, but a real friend who sticks closer than a brother is better.

Before we continue, let's take a moment and seriously pray together. We need to cry out to God:

God, wake us up! Give us a revelation of true friendship and fellowship! Restore Your plan for our families. Set us free from screens. Give us a heart tattoo so we can burn for You! In Jesus' name we pray. Amen!

As a pastor, I've been with people at the end of their life on this earth. I've never heard any of them say, "Bring my phone to my bedside. I want to scroll through my Facebook and Instagram feeds one more time before I die." No one says that. They say things like, "I want to see my brother [or my cousin or my friend or a family member] one more time before I die."

Reader, what I want you to know is that you don't have to wait until you get to the end of your life on this earth to realize what matters most: relationships, family and friends!

If your screen has become a drug to you, please ask for help. Don't get me wrong, I appreciate all the blessings with technology, but for some of you, it's destroying you!

The early believers were devoted to each other. They were willing to lay down their lives for each other, just as Jesus did for them. They weren't fair-weather friends; they were faithful to each other.

Church wasn't a slice of their weekly pie; it was the foundation of their new lives. Church wasn't something they did only one day a week; they did *life* together. Fellowship mattered to them, and it made all the difference.

FELLOWSHIP AND FRIENDSHIP MAKE ALL THE DIFFERENCE

Some time ago, a young man from our youth group was changing schools. He expressed his worries and fears to me, his youth pastor at the time. He was nervous about meeting new people, fitting in and making friends. I know that change like this can be difficult, so I touched base with him after his first week to see how things were going. He responded, saying, "Travis! It's going pretty good so far." And then he said words that still bring tears to my eyes: "I have a friend who sits with me at lunch!"

If you can say, *"I have a friend,"* you can face anything.

Having a friend—having *fellowship*—makes all the difference in the world when going through changes in life. Fellowship helps us persevere in the face of fear. I believe a friend is one of the greatest things you can be in this life.

People pursue a lot of things in life that don't really matter. Do you want to do something that matters in life? Be a friend. Everyone needs a friend. Everyone needs fellowship.

> *"As iron sharpens iron, so a friend sharpens a friend."*
> *(Proverbs 27:17)*

GOD'S PRESCRIPTION FOR FEAR

Following Jesus isn't all peaches-and-cream. Jesus said the narrow road would be difficult. (See Matthew 7:14.) I'm grateful that Jesus didn't candy-coat the gospel, as many preachers do today. Don't get me wrong, following Jesus is sweet, but it's also hard. You will have some tough days.

Here's an example of the apostle Paul sharing honestly about the tough days:

> *"When we arrived in Macedonia, there was no rest for us. We faced conflict from every direction, with battles on the outside and fear on the inside. But God, who encourages those who are discouraged, encouraged us by the arrival of Titus." (2 Corinthians 7:5–6)*

I love Paul's vulnerability here. Tired and worn down from the external fight and internal fears of doing what God called him to do, Paul shares how God strengthens and encourages us by showing up in times like this.

When faced with exterior battles and internal fears, what does God prescribe?

One word: Titus!

Paul was a mentor to Titus. Here, we see a beautiful example of iron sharpening iron. Here, we see that discipleship relationships are a two-way street. Here, we see a beautiful picture of godly friendship. Here, we see Paul needing Titus, just as Titus needed Paul.

Fair-weather friends are nowhere to be found when the road gets difficult. Titus wasn't a fair-weather friend; he was a faithful friend.

God's prescription for breaking us free from fear and discouragement is to send us a friend. Not drugs or alcohol or sex, but a *friend*. Not Netflix or Hulu or Disney+, but a *friend*. Not Facebook or YouTube or Twitter, but a *friend*.

When you walk through tough times with a friend, your bond grows stronger and your appreciation for the relationship increases. This is the opportunity in the storm.

God's way of encouraging Paul, and those traveling with him, was to send Titus. He does the same thing today. You are someone's Titus when you are in the body of Christ.

A friend makes all the difference in the world when you are going through trials and storms in life. A brother or a sister in the faith is one of the greatest encouragers we can have. The presence of a friend breaks off fear and refreshes the soul. This can happen in Macedonia and it can happen at a lunch table. God deals with fear through the gift of friendship. This is something we all need.

EVERYONE NEEDS A FRIEND

During my addiction, I felt so alone. That feeling gripped me every day, and I know a lot of people feel the same way. So, one thing I like to do is hit the streets and talk to people. I believe in all my heart that *conversations are suicide prevention.* So many people live with thoughts of *Nobody cares!* running through their minds. When you can get your eyes off yourself, your screen, and your agenda, and simply consider the needs of others by sparking conversations with them, that lie can no longer remain because someone just cared for them. Every act of love is an act of war. Conversations with others shield them from the enemy's arrows of lies and accusations. Many people are literally one arrow away from a suicide attempt. We thwart the enemy's plans through *consideration* and *conversation.* People will stay alive if you simply say, "Hi."

Stop for a moment and feel the weight of that.

One day, as I was out loving on people, I had just finished praying with a guy and was walking back to my truck when I saw another gentleman walking across the street. I said, "Hello, sir. How are you?" He looked at me and, with an attitude, asked, "Do I know you?" I replied, "I am not sure. You look familiar. What's your name?" He told me his name and I asked him what he was up to, but my questions and attempts to start a conversation received only one-word answers.

Then, he asked me a question with a suspicious countenance, "What are you doing? Are you just going around talking to people?"

In that moment, and still to this very day, his question hit me like a brick of sadness.

"Are you just going around talking to people?"

As his words moved from my head to my heart, I felt his pain. This was my question in response: "People don't do that, do they?"

With anger etched across his face, he replied, "No! People don't do that."

I could tell by his response that it had been a long time since he had received a simple "hello." He was so suspicious and paranoid that, at one point, he even asked if I was a probation officer.

Mother Teresa once said, "The most terrible poverty is loneliness and the feeling of being unloved."

HERE ARE MY QUESTIONS FOR YOU:

What if you turn off the news for an hour and love your neighbor? What if you ask the cashier how she is doing instead of complaining about how long the line is? What if you pray instead of having an argument about the President? What if you take your eyes off the screen and sit with someone in need? What if you live by the words of Jesus when He said, "Deny yourself, take up your cross and follow me." (See Matthew 16:24 NKJV). What if?

Maybe it would be an end to loneliness, isolation, depression and suicide. Maybe it would save your child, your father, your grandmother, your brother or sister from feeling alone.

Jesus said to His disciples,

> *"You are the light of the world—like a city on a hilltop that cannot be hidden. No one lights a lamp and then puts it under a basket. Instead, a lamp is placed on a stand, where it gives light to everyone in the house. In the same way, let your good deeds shine out for all to see, so that everyone will praise your heavenly Father." (Matthew 5:14–16)*

Jesus came to destroy the works of the devil. (See 1 John 3:8.) Loneliness is one of those works. Shining His light destroys it. Considering the wellbeing of others destroys it.

If we're going to see a decline in overdoses, suicides, loneliness and depression, then Christians need to remove the baskets from their heads and shine the light of God's redeeming love into the world of the lost and lonely. One encounter with the King can change everything. One conversation, one prayer, one acknowledgement, one prophetic word, one act of kindness and generosity can turn someone's life around.

This verse is still God's desire for the way in which He partners with us:

> *"God places the lonely in families; he sets the prisoners free and gives them joy." (Psalm 68:6)*

From *lonely* to *family*. From *family* to *freedom*. From *freedom* to *joy*. God's solution for ending loneliness is family, and in the context of family, He sets prisoners free and gives them joy. You won't find real freedom and joy outside of God's family.

Everyone needs a friend. Maybe we should start by saying, "Hi." If we work together, we will change the world by changing someone's world.

Mother Teresa also said, "I alone cannot change the world, but I can cast a stone across the waters to create many ripples."

Conversations create ripples, and ripples precede revival.

TOGETHER

The word for *fellowship* in Greek is *koinonia.* One of the meanings for *koinonia* is "joint participation." When you have true fellowship (*koinonia*) you have joint participation in the cause of Christ with other believers. United in the Spirit and by the Spirit, you live daily to strengthen each other and to shine as lights in this dark world. Our fellowship with each other reveals the love of Jesus to the world. Our relationships with each other should reveal Jesus.

When Jesus said to His disciples, *"You are the light of the world"* (Matthew 5:14), He was saying, in essence, *"Together,* you are the light. *Together,* you'll reveal Me to the world."

Jesus also put it this way:

> *"A new commandment I give to you, that you love one another, even as I have loved you, that you also love one another. By this all men will know that you are My disciples, if you have love for one another." (John 13:34–35 NASB)*

All men will know that we belong to Jesus if we love each other. Our relationships, how we treat each other, are a message that speaks to the world. If Jesus is at the center of our relationships and our main Connector, the way we walk together will be the most powerful sermon the church ever shares with the world.

To gain a real devotion to fellowship, we must first shatter a couple of lies.

. . .

LIE #1: "I'M BETTER OFF ALONE."

"Then the Lord God said, "It is not good for the man to be alone." (Genesis 2:18)

At first, being lost in New York City was fun for Kevin McCallister. I love the movie *Home Alone 2.* (I'll bet you didn't see that coming.) Staying at a sweet hotel filled with lots of goodies and a pocketful of cash made it seem as though Kevin found true freedom at last. With toy stores, cheese pizza and limousine rides, Kevin was finally living the high life. With no more pressure from Mom and Dad or his brother Buzz, Kevin could finally do whatever he wanted.

Often in life, because of family pain and relational struggle, people believe the lie that they would be better off alone. Many people's defense to being hurt is to isolate. But here's the truth: isolated pain is never healed; it only gets worse. No one is meant to go through life alone. God is about family and relationships, not about isolation and separation. If emotional pain has you alone and on the run, turn around and run into the arms of Jesus. There is no wound too deep for Him to heal.

It didn't take long for Kevin to learn two powerful truths:

1. **Without the protection of family, you're more vulnerable to the enemy**. Marv and Harry, the bad guys, found Kevin alone outside Duncan's Toy Chest, and in a moment, Kevin went from having fun to running from danger. If the enemy can disconnect you, he can destroy you. We only have two choices: disconnect and be destroyed or remain connected to fellowship and conquer.

This passage has become sweet music to my soul:

"Two people are better off than one, for they can help each other succeed. If one person falls, the other can reach out and help. But someone who falls alone is in real trouble. Likewise, two people lying close together can keep each other warm. But how can one be warm alone? A person standing alone can be attacked and defeated, but two can stand back-to-back and conquer. Three are even better, for a triple-braided cord is not easily broken." (Ecclesiastes 4:9–12)

2. **Only in quiet can you hear the cry of the heart**. Alone at night in his hotel room, Kevin's heart began to cry out for his mom. His heart wasn't crying out for more money, more junk or more toys, but for his mom and family. Kevin didn't really want to be alone, and neither do you. This truth was revealed in stillness.

"Be still, and know that I am God!" (Psalm 46:10)

Stop hiding in the noise of life and *be still* so that truth can be revealed. Your busyness is burying you. Your constant activity is fueled by the enemy, and his purpose is to keep you bound by keeping you isolated and on the move. It's time to put an end to isolation and move toward reconciliation. "Better off alone" is a lie!

One of my favorite scenes in *Home Alone 2* is when Mr. Duncan gives Kevin the two turtledoves. This gift was given to Kevin because of his generosity and the financial blessing he was able to give to the kids in the children's home.

This is what Mr. Duncan said when Kevin asked about the turtledoves:

I'll tell you what you do. You keep one and you give the other one to a very special person. You see, turtledoves are a symbol of friendship and love. And as long as each of you has your turtledove, you'll be friends forever.

God will always remind us of our need for each other. He cares deeply about the gift of friendship, fellowship and family. We all need to receive a turtledove, and we all have a turtledove to give.

Someone today is waiting on you to pass the dove. Someone today is waiting on you to say, "Hi."

> *"Don't let these wild beasts destroy your turtledoves. Don't forget your suffering people forever." (Psalm 74:19)*

LIE #2: "I HAVE 'MY' RELATIONSHIP WITH GOD."

I've heard a lot of people say things like, "I don't need to go to church to have a relationship with God" or "My church is in the woods."

Really? Do me a favor. Read those statements a few more times, slowly.

These are statements of control, not surrender, to the Lordship of King Jesus. "I don't need…" and "My church…". These words reveal that *you* are still Lord of your life and that you haven't actually *given* your life to Jesus.

What did you get saved from?

Jesus never said, "Follow me and then do your own thing." His motto wasn't that of Burger King. Jesus never said, "Have it your way." Here is what Jesus said:

> *"Then Jesus said to his disciples, "If any of you wants to be*

my follower, you must give up your own way, take up your
cross, and follow me." (Matthew 16:24)

Have you given up your "own way"? Your way is not *the way*!

You can't have a connection with Christ and not desire to be connected to others. It's true that we all need personal time with the Lord. I like to spend time in nature too, as I will touch on in Section 4, but it's also important to have times of fellowship with others. If Christ is truly in you, fellowship time with others will matter to you.

Going to church, joining a small group, seeking opportunities to serve and become involved, hitting the streets to share the love of God with others and connecting with fellow believers who can pray and look out for you can radically transform your life and wellbeing. God designed us to need each other for a reason. Standing back-to-back with another believer keeps the enemy from attacking your blind spot. When you have a friend, you never have to stay down.

Refuse to allow pride to keep you in isolation. Don't fall for a make-believe version of Christianity that is more about personal comfort than being vulnerable and actually following Christ.

I love seeing God move in my life, but I also love it when I see others encounter Him. It is time to break free from both of these lies. There is nothing better about being alone. If the message you receive from your time spent in the woods is telling you that you don't need to connect with others, you are not hearing from Jesus in those woods!

Ponder these two verses:

"Let us think of ways to motivate one another to acts of love

and good works. And let us not neglect our meeting together, as some people do, but encourage one another, especially now that the day of his return is drawing near." (Hebrews 10:24–25)

WITHOUT FELLOWSHIP, WE CAN'T FULLY KNOW GOD

Kelsey and I have been together for eleven years and married for seven. Our relationship began when she heard about me through a coworker who was basically like family to me. This person described me as someone whose life was turned around. (Side note for singles: you don't have to sell yourself; let God speak for you.)

It was this conversation that led Kelsey to message me. Now, I'm going to show my age a little, but the message was sent through Myspace. Long story short, I saw this message a few weeks later and it led to a phone conversation, which led to a few more phone conversations, which led to our first "dinner and a movie date."

That's how our relationship got started. It was in the conversations, phone calls, and date nights that we were able to form a connection with each other. You need one-on-one time to truly get to know someone. Those first dates are where the flames of love first sparked; but then the time came for me to meet her best friends.

It was at a Fourth of July fireworks celebration that I got to see a side of Kelsey I hadn't seen before—her *friend side*. A goofiness and sense of humor that would've stayed hidden had we stayed alone now came to the surface. Seeing her interact with her friends helped me to better understand who she is, which caused me to fall more in love with her.

After that, the time came for me to meet her family. That was when I got to see her *big sister side* and her *daughter side*, which revealed other facets of who Kelsey is. And the love kept growing.

It is the same in our relationship with God. If you remain alone with God, you'll miss out on fully knowing Him. Fellowship time with others reveals more facets of our beautiful Bridegroom King.

Some people say things like, "I like Jesus; I just don't like people." This is impossible.

> *"Anyone who does not love does not know God, for God is love." (1 John 4:8)*

> *"If someone says, "I love God," but hates a fellow believer, that person is a liar; for if we don't love people we can see, how can we love God, whom we cannot see?" (verse 20)*

If you don't like, or if perhaps you even *hate*, people, *you don't know Jesus*. You might know religion, you might know "churchianity," but you don't know Jesus. If that is *you*, it's time to forgive. Jesus will help you and heal you. His love is going to wash over you!

Stop for a moment and cry out to Him! Ask Jesus to help you forgive and to heal your hurts. He wants to do this because He loves you!

I love one-on-one time with the Lord, but again, I also love to see what Jesus is doing in the lives of my friends and family. Hearing about their faith helps me to better see the fuller beauty of who God is. When I experience His love in the secret place, I always leave with a desire to share His love with others. Isolation is the last thing on my mind after an intimate time of prayer and worship. Resentment is the last thing on my mind after time in the Word. I always leave the secret place with a burning desire to share His love with others. It's too good not to share.

There's more to learn about who God is in His fullness. It's found in the secret place, but also in the place of fellowship with others. We all need both. My friends help to reveal more of who God is to me.

All the testimonies and encounters with God in the Bible reveal who God is in His fullness. Every parable Jesus tells reveals more of who God is. Every testimony of God's love at work in someone's life reveals another facet of who God is.

You will miss facets of Jesus if you isolate and do your own thing. If you've been hurt, remember that Jesus can heal. We need each other. Don't let unforgiveness rob you of the gift of fellowship.

FACETS OF JESUS REVEALED IN THE STORIES OF OTHERS

Let's check out a few biblical examples:

- Mary Magdalene: Her story reveals the delivering power of God. (See Luke 8:2.)
- Peter: His story reveals the patience of God, and how He never stops believing in us. (See Luke 22:31–32.)
- Zacchaeus: His story reveals that even if others hate you, God will still help you. (See Luke 19:1–10.)
- Saul (who became the apostle Paul: His story reveals a God who counts no one out. Saul's story reveals the God of surprise. (See Acts 9.)
- Lois and Eunice: Their story shows us the

importance of teaching God's Word to our children. I like to call it "parental discipleship." It is God's desire for us to train up our kids in the way they should go. Prayer and Bible study in the home matters to God. (See 2 Timothy 1:5.)

- John, the apostle: His story reveals the God who desires friendship and intimacy. (See John 13:23.)

I could go on and on. Please take time and read those passages, even if you have read them before.

These are only a few examples, but I want you to see that through each of these individual stories, we see more facets of who Jesus is. Again, take time to read those passages and fall more in love with Jesus. If you isolate yourself from others, you'll miss out on seeing all facets of who Jesus is. Each of the stories makes me fall more in love with the Lord and fills me with hope and encouragement.

It's important to remember that others need to hear your story as well. Your testimony can be the key that sets a captive free. It's time for selfishness to end. It's time to stop hiding in the woods. Let's look at the solution for ending selfishness.

NO FIRE/NO FELLOWSHIP

"On the day of Pentecost all the believers were meeting together in one place. Suddenly, there was a sound from heaven like the roaring of a mighty windstorm, and it filled the house where they were sitting. Then, what looked like flames or tongues of fire appeared and settled on each of them. And everyone present was filled with the Holy Spirit

and began speaking in other languages, as the Holy Spirit gave them this ability." (Acts 2:1–4)

After the Holy Spirit was poured out and the fire fell on the day of Pentecost, the community was formed. Around three thousand people were saved and baptized. Many call Pentecost the birthday of the church. The fire fell, the Word was preached, hearts were pierced and sinners were set free when they repented and believed. First fire, then true fellowship.

NO FIRE OF THE HOLY SPIRIT = NO FELLOWSHIP WITH OTHERS

FIRE PURIFIES AND DESTROYS SELFISHNESS. Selfishness is the enemy of true fellowship because selfishness hinders service. You can't have joint participation if you're selfish. When you're baptized in the Holy Spirt through turning to God in repentance, you are filled with God. To be filled with God is to be filled with good.

Here's the fruit of the fire:

> *"And all the believers met **together** in one place and **shared** everything they had. They sold their property and possessions and **shared** the money with those in need. They worshiped **together** at the Temple each day, **met in homes** for the Lord's Supper, and **shared** their meals with great joy and **generosity**—all the while praising God and enjoying the goodwill of all the people. And each day the Lord added to their fellowship those who were being saved." (Acts 2:44–47, emphasis added)*

We see in this passage that *sharing* with others is a clear fruit of being baptized with the Holy Spirit and with fire. When you are consumed by the Holy Spirit, *selflessness* replaces *selfishness*.

When it comes to talking about the baptism of the Holy Spirit, however, many focus on speaking in tongues or another gift or manifestation of the Spirit as the evidence of being filled. I do believe those are evidence, but so is *sharing* and *selflessness*, and they should be talked about as well. The fire that fell even caused those earlier believers to share their money. *Can you believe that?*

If you talk in tongues, pray in the spirit and prophesy but remain mean and selfish, you might just be *religious*. All the gifts and manifestations of the Spirit are beautiful and needed. They are not to be abused or hidden behind. The Holy Spirt manifests in many powerful ways, and I am thankful for all of them, but He also gets up in our business and confronts hidden motives and selfish agendas. Don't speak in tongues but keep your hard heart. Don't prophesy on Sunday but lie to others on Monday. Let the Holy Spirt do a deep work in you so that Jesus can be seen through you. This strengthens the fellowship, which is what all the gifts are supposed to do.

A connection must be made with God through our surrender to Him. Then we can truly connect with others on a deeply spiritual level. When there's no vertical connection and receiving of God's love, there's no horizontal connection and giving of God's love. Only when we have a connection with Jesus can we experience joint participation with others. If we allow the Holy Spirit to work in us, He will burn away every divider. Let Him fill you and consume you continually. When individual flames connect, revival fire spreads. Remember this: one flame can light millions of other flames.

If fellowship is born from fire, then fellowship should be warm. The lost and weary are looking for the warmth of love. Those frozen by fear are looking to fiery lovers for freedom. Heat draws the cold like sinners were drawn to Jesus. Remember, one can't be warm all alone.

It's time to become devoted to true fellowship with other believers. It's time to become set on fire so that the fellowship of the Lord grows and we see the lost come home.

Fellowship born from fire becomes a powerful magnet of the love of God, empowered by the Holy Spirit, which draws the lost into God's family. The Lord adds to this kind of fellowship.

One time, a friend from my past visited our church. Later that same evening, he sent me a message, saying, "I don't know what it is, but I feel this love pulling me there."

The Lord does add to fellowships that *share* His love, and He also calls us to *go!*

Jesus said,

> *"But you will receive power when the Holy Spirit comes upon you. And you will be my witnesses, telling people about me everywhere—in Jerusalem, throughout Judea, in Samaria, and to the ends of the earth." (Acts 1:8)*

FELLOWSHIP GROWS WHEN WE *GO FISH*!

Jesus called out to them, "Come, follow me, and I will show you how to fish for people!" (Matthew 4:19)

One of my favorite card games to play as a child was Go Fish. I hadn't played it in years, but the Holy Spirit kept telling me, "Look up the directions to Go Fish." The game is simple but fun. One player asks another player if they have a certain card. If they don't have the card, they respond by saying, "Go fish." That player will then grab a card from a pool of other cards, with the goal of making a set.

The pool of cards is swirled around face down in a mess so they can't be identified. Cards then leave the messy pool to be united with others when a player selects them for their hand. These cards go from being lost in a messy pool to being held in someone's hands. Imagine that your life is a card in that messy pool, and someone chooses not to leave you there.

Many people are face down in a mess, and we, as the body of Christ, are called to Go Fish. The messes of life cause people to lose sight of their true identities and purpose. The shame of sin has left a lot of people hanging their heads. If we, who are in God's hands, don't step out and become His helping hands, others will remain lost, stuck face down in a mess. But when we reach down and pull them out, they will no longer be lost, but found.

Go Fish! Get close to the mess, reach in and pull them out! Someone today can be held in God's hands if you reach out your hand. Someone today can feel the warmth of God's love if we extend our hand to help. Someone today can find hope in their heart through a hug with your arms.

Jesus wants His family to grow; He wants none to perish. That's why we are called to help pull them away from the flames of judgement.

"Rescue others by snatching them from the flames of judgment." (Jude 23)

God trains us as His disciples to fish for men and women. It's an amazing feeling when, with your own eyes, you see someone come out of darkness and into His marvelous light. Fishing grows the fellowship, and right now, the world is full of opportunities. In fact, it's a "honey hole."

HONEY HOLES

In fishing terminology, a "honey hole" is a particular spot in a body of water (or perhaps an entire body of water) in which conditions are ideal for catching fish.

God spoke to me through a prophetic dream on August 7, 2019. He told me that right now, my community, and America in general, is a honey hole for the kingdom. The conditions are ideal for reaching the lost. There's a hunger for something real, for something that truly satisfies the soul's thirst. If we cast the Bread of Life (Jesus Christ) into the sin-filled streets of our communities, people will get hooked on the truth and be reeled into the Savior's arms. Jesus is ready to reel people out of the dark waters of sin and into the living waters of new life. And He wants to use *you* to do so.

[Jesus said,] "The true bread of God is the one who comes down from Heaven and gives life to the world." "Sir," they said, "give us that bread every day." Jesus replied, "I am the bread of life. Whoever comes to me will never be hungry again. Whoever believes in me will never be thirsty." (John 6:33–35)

It's time to increase our seed-planting and watering. There is an increase of salvations coming, if we do our part. Come on, laborers. Let's get into the field and see the revival of our communities and of the world.

When you follow Jesus, He makes you a fisher of men. Reaching the lost isn't just something we do, it's who we are. I am a fisher of men. It's a part of my DNA now that I'm a disciple of Jesus.

FELLOWSHIP GROWS AFTER FISHERS OF MEN "GO"!

For a fish to get hooked, bait must be cast. For the lost to be found, they need to know about the One who is searching for them. We, as the body of Christ, are to be the hands and feet of Jesus. For people to leave their old lives, they must see that a new life is possible.

Fish don't naturally swim to fishermen; a fisherman goes to where the fish are and offers them something different.

Your community isn't a hellhole. America isn't a hellhole. The world isn't a hellhole; it's a honey hole, and the conditions are ideal for reaching the lost. If we seize this opportunity, we will change the atmosphere and trajectory of our neighborhoods in ways that will move in ripples into the world. Revival becomes a reality when we obey the Word of the Lord. I believe the Lord is highlighting Ephesians 5 in this season:

> "Be careful how you live. Don't live like fools, but like those who are wise. Make the most of every opportunity in these evil days. Don't act thoughtlessly, but understand what the Lord wants you to do." (Ephesians 5:15–17)

Everyone who truly lives for Jesus will lead people to Jesus. Not through human effort but by living transformed lives. If you're fishing and not getting any bites, you're not casting Jesus. The broken have always been drawn to Jesus. Empty hooks don't catch fish, just as loveless churchgoers don't reach the lost.

What's on your hook?

What are you offering the world around you?

To fish some honey holes, fishermen must put on waders, get into the water and walk to the hot spot. We, as followers of Jesus, are to walk into the world as carriers of the hope found in the fire of the Holy Spirit, casting the Light of the world into every dark corner.

Darkness is the ideal condition for every Christian to fulfill the great commission. We don't run from darkness; we run into darkness and watch it flee.

Waders are *waterproof* boots that allow you to fish in cold conditions. It's important to know that the Holy Spirit makes us *world-proof*. To be world-proof is to live every day under the influence of the Holy Spirit. When you are under His influence, you're no longer subject to the influences of this world. This is the recipe for reaching the lost. It's true! You can live unspotted (uncorrupted) by the world. (See James 1:27.) The only hope for a cold world is a church on fire.

> *"Don't be drunk with wine, because that will ruin your life. Instead, be filled with the Holy Spirit, singing psalms and hymns and spiritual songs among yourselves, and making music to the Lord in your hearts. And give thanks for everything to God the Father in the name of our Lord Jesus Christ." (Ephesians 5:18–20)*

Into the coldness of the world, we are to cast Christ. The conditions are ideal. The forecast calls for revival. What are you waiting for?

It's time for His fellowship to grow! *Let's go!*

A FRIEND FOR LIFE

On Sunday afternoon a few years ago, I was driving home from church when I saw a man sitting at the bus stop with a couple of suitcases and two pillows. The Holy Spirt gave me a nudge and said, "Stop and talk to the man."

I parked my truck and started up the sidewalk, communing with Jesus the whole time. When I got to the man, he was looking down at his cellphone. I said, "Hi, how are you today?" He looked up, and with straight-up honesty, said, "I'm not good." I introduced myself and sat down beside him.

When you live a Spirit-led life, it's always fishing time.

Have you ever had a rough night when you made some terrible decisions? I am talking about a dark night of the soul, when you wake up hating yourself, feeling helpless and hopeless. That is what this man was going through. He poured out his heart to me and shared his pain. I listened, identifying with him 100 percent. I had been in that place before. I was in that place when Jesus rescued me. Drugs and alcohol had brought him to an all-time low and he had been kicked out of his family's home. He was waiting for a bus to take him to Baltimore, wondering if he would ever see his kids again. He was sitting there, being pounded by lies from the enemy and feeling worthless. As I listened to him, God began speaking things to my heart. This is what the Lord had me share with him: "I was just heading home from church.

As I drove by, I saw you sitting here, and Jesus told me to stop and see how you were doing."

Before I even finished the sentence, he lost it. He began to cry, and I just held him in my arms and spoke life into him as he trembled through the tears.

Then, after I told him some of my personal story, I said, "God is trying to get your attention. He's knocking on the door of your heart. You should let Him in. Jesus loves you."

As he held out both of His hands, I asked, "Are you ready?" With tears rolling down his cheeks, he said, "Yeah." In this posture of surrender, he gave Jesus his life. Immediately, he was filled with peace and fresh hope. With my own eyes, I watched the darkness flee as the light of God's love was turned on in this man's life.

After we prayed, He kept saying, "This is crazy, man. This is crazy, man." Then he started repeating, "You're never going to believe this. You're never going to believe this." With great excitement, I was thinking, *I'm going to believe this, I'm a believer.*

He started scrolling through his phone and pulled up a text message he had sent to his kids' mother an hour before. In the message, he had said this: "I'm going to turn my life over to God, and things are going to change and I'm going to get better."

Yeah, Jesus! Glory Hallelujah! My jaw was on the floor.

One hour after he had sent that message, Jesus had me driving by and gave me a nudge, all in response to this man's text-message prayer. That is why it's important that we never neglect those nudges. Children of God are all called to live available lives, ready to be used by our Master for His good work. Jesus reeled in my new friend that day. He pulled him out of the hopeless waters of the world and into His loving arms.

God does hear us. God does speak to us. God heard that man's prayer and wanted to give him an opportunity to truly surrender. He wasn't mad at the man. He wanted to help; He wanted to break his chains. If this dude was confused about how real and personal Jesus is, I promise you he wasn't confused anymore. He was awestruck by our awesome God.

At one point in our conversation, he told me that he had been sitting at that bus stop all night and hadn't eaten. I crossed the street to a Subway to grab him a sandwich. While I was getting his food, his bus pulled up. The sandwich makers hurried and I was able to give the man his food before his bus headed off to Baltimore. He was so grateful. I'll never forget his smile.

Before getting on the bus, I gave him my phone number and he said to me, "Travis, when you first sat down, I was about to ask you for some weed." We just laughed as we went our separate ways, but after I got in my truck, I really thought about his words.

It's pretty powerful that he forgot to ask me for some weed. He was hurting when I first stopped, still looking to numb the pain the only way he knew how. But when Jesus meets your needs, you no longer need weed. He was no longer empty. He was filled with the presence of God. He wasn't stuck face down in a mess anymore. God chose him to be on His team. When you get filled with the *right thing*, you no longer need the *wrong things*. He forgot to ask me for some weed because He no longer needed it. When you have a friend, you can face anything. Godly fellowship will keep you out of the devil's grip.

The Most High is greater than a weed high. Amen!

He sent me a text message about an hour later, saying, "Thank you for stopping. You got a friend for life, bro!"

Friendship, fellowship, family and fishing matters!

It's time to come out of isolation. It's time to stop neglecting nudges. It's time to forgive. It's time to heal. It's time to get back to church. It's time to say, "Hi." It's time to pass the dove. It's time to learn how to love. It's time to get your eyes off the screen. It's time to help. It's time to hug. It's time to get a heart tattoo. It's time to serve. It's time to give.

It's time to truly live!

3

SECTION 3: DEVOTION TO COMMUNION

"Recognize in this bread what hung on the cross, and in this chalice what flowed from His side."—St. Augustine

The third component of the awe factor is a devotion to communion, the Lord's Supper. Communion is more than just having a snack at a church service. Communion is about taking time to remember what Christ did for us on the cross, as well as a time to reflect on our lives in the light of His love. The bread and the juice are to help connect our hearts and minds to the passion of Jesus and His love for us, so that we never forget it.

Communion is a two-sided coin. One side is *remembrance*; the other side is *reflection*. We will start this section with *remembrance*.

*"He took some bread and gave thanks to God for it. Then he broke it in pieces and gave it to the disciples, saying, "This is my body, which is given for you. **Do this in remembrance of me.**" After supper he took another cup of wine and said, "This cup is the new covenant between God and his people —an agreement confirmed with my blood, which is poured*

out as a sacrifice for you." (Luke 22:19–20, emphasis added)

DO THIS IN REMEMBRANCE OF ME

Jesus said, *"Do this in remembrance of me."*

God's people have had a long history of forgetting Him. God would rescue them, things would get better in their lives, and then they would go back to living for themselves. Sadly, they always ended up in trouble again. This was a vicious cycle. God helped them, they forgot, and, inevitably, they ended up in a horrible mess again.

As an example, here is God speaking through the prophet Hosea:

> *"I have been the Lord your God ever since I brought you out of Egypt. You must acknowledge no God but me, for there is no other savior. I took care of you in the wilderness, in that dry and thirsty land. But when you had eaten and were satisfied, you became proud and forgot me." (Hosea 13:4)*

After God met the Israelites' needs, they became full of pride and forgot the fact that they never would've made it out of Egypt without His intervention. They forgot that it was God who had brought them out. They forgot that it was God who had sustained them in the wilderness. This is why pride is so dangerous.

I've been to the funerals of people who forgot God. Prisons and jails all over the world all filled with people who forgot God. Families have been broken and children have been abandoned because of parents who forgot God. Graveyards all over the world are filled with the bones of people who forgot God. They missed the life that God had for them. Hell is also full of people who forgot God. Forgetting God isn't a game or a light issue. Heed this warning:

> *"Pride goes before destruction, and haughtiness before a fall." (Proverbs 16:18)*

Through communion, I believe that one of Jesus's desires is to break this unhealthy cycle. We don't have to be trapped in this rat race; we can be connected to Christ and live in freedom. We don't have to remain stuck on hell's hamster wheel; we can live lives that are led by the Holy Spirit. We don't have to go back to Egypt; we can abide in the vine (see John 15) and live in victory.

A MESSAGE FOR JOHN

I have a message for John. Do you know John? John was a friend of Bill.

Maybe this will help…

Now, John at the bar is a friend of mine; He gets me my drinks for free.

And he's quick with a joke or to light up your smoke,

But there's someplace that he'd rather be.

He says, "Bill, I believe this is killing me,"

As the smile ran away from his face.

"Well, I'm sure that I could be a movie star, if I could get out of this place."

These are lyrics from the song "Piano Man," written and performed by Billy Joel and released in 1973. The song was based on Joel's own experience as a piano lounge-singer for six months between 1972–1973. All the characters in the song are based on real people.

I don't know about you, but I can relate to John. Maybe you're like John, or maybe you know a John. If I were to sit down with the Johns of the world, this is what I would say:

Thanks for your honesty, John. Thanks for being real. Honesty is the beginning of change.

And then I would say,

John, you can get out of this place. You can't do it in your own strength, but you can get out of this place. Your dream doesn't have to die, John. It's time to stop hiding behind jokes and get serious, because this lifestyle is killing you.

You weren't born to be trapped in a barroom, John. God put a dream in you. Jesus has a plan for you. Your smile ran away because you are outside of God's will for your life. Jesus died on the cross so that every outsider could come home. That invitation is for you too, John. Stop listening to the devil's lies and give your life to Christ. Call out to Him for help and He will pull you out. Jesus loves you, John, and He wants to help you. You can get out of this place and stay out of this place, with God's help.

Maybe you're not stuck in a bar like John was. Maybe you're stuck in an abusive relationship and you feel trapped. Maybe you're bound in an addiction like I was, and you've lost all hope. Maybe you're stuck in the pain of your past. I thought I would die with a needle in my arm, but God brought me out and, through a daily relationship with Him, He has kept me out. And now, a big part of what God has called me to do is to let the Johns of the world know the way out. *Jesus is the way.*

You can get out of that abusive relationship and stay out of that abusive relationship. *Real love doesn't make you black and blue.*

You can get out of jail and stay out of jail. *Orange isn't your color, anyway.*

You can get clean from drugs and alcohol and you can stay clean from drugs and alcohol. *Overdose isn't your destiny.*

You can get out of debt and stay out of debt. *Financial freedom is possible through Christ.*

There's no chain too thick that Jesus can't break it.

Then I would say to John, "Keep reading, bro!"

GET OUT AND STAY OUT

> *"He lifted me out of the pit of despair, out of the mud and the mire. He set my feet on solid ground and steadied me as I walked along." (Psalm 40:2)*

David so beautifully captures this powerful truth: you can get out and stay out!

God will pull you out of the mud and the mire. He will bring you up from the bottom of your brokenness when you ask for help and will place you on solid ground. And then, to keep you from slipping back into the mud, He will steady you as you walk along. Jesus wants to hold your hand.

People who slip back into the mud stopped surrendering to the steadying of the Lord. They let go of His hand. They forgot God. They proclaimed, "I got this!" You're in danger when you think, *I got this!* We need Jesus to get out and stay out.

Even after the mud is removed, it's important to remember the mud from which you were rescued. If you don't remember the mud, the pain, the hurt, the sin, the bondage and the abuse, you'll end up getting stuck in it again. If you don't remember your Rescuer, you'll need to be rescued again.

Here's the good news: you can't slip if you're living in God's grip. When you're holding His hand, He's holding you with His strength. A regular practice of communion tightens the grip and deepens your love for the One who pulled you out. If we are regularly remembering what Jesus did for us on the cross, and the crushing of His body leading up to it, we will never live unloved lives.

When people live with the mindset that they are unloved, they open themselves up to all kinds of evil. The lie called "unloved" is planted by the enemy to make you vulnerable to his schemes. Temptations that, at one time, never even came onto your radar suddenly begin to look more attractive when bound by this stronghold. That is why communion is so important. It keeps you free from this lie because you are staying locked-in on God's love for you.

You are loved, and when you remember how loved you are, you'll stop looking for love in all the wrong places. Love doesn't come from money, sex, drugs or rock and roll. Love comes from God.

Here's your next heart tattoo: *Love Comes from God!*

"Dear friends, let us continue to love one another, for love

comes from God. Anyone who loves is a child of God and knows God." (1 John 4:7)

Because of the cross, we can go directly to the source of love. Jesus's love tank never runs dry. Therefore, no one needs to go through life empty of love ever again. Communion keeps us full of the love of God.

Taking communion also keeps unhealthy doors shut. When you remember that Jesus was beaten so that you could be made whole, and that His blood was poured out so that you could be forgiven and free, you will no longer be a sitting duck for the enemy. (See Isaiah 53.)

A sitting duck is someone who is easy pickings for an enemy attack. Sitting ducks are easy targets for bird hunters, much as complacent Christians are to the devil.

Peter warned us about this:

"Stay alert! Watch out for your great enemy, the devil. He prowls around like a roaring lion, looking for someone to devour." (1 Peter 5:8)

Hunters know that birds in flight are harder to shoot. A bird sitting on a body of water is much easier to shoot than a bird flying in the air. Communion keeps you soaring on the wings of God's love. Communion will help you remain focused on the assignment the Lord has for your life. When you practice communion, you won't slip into complacency. You'll be too busy soaring into your destiny.

"If a bird sees a trap being set, it knows to stay away." (Proverbs 1:17)

Not having a devotion to communion is a trap every believer needs to stay away from. The trap of pride and self-sufficiency awaits those who forget God. Communion is a pride-crusher. It takes your eyes off yourself and on Christ.

Jesus knew that we, like the Israelites, can be quick forgetters. Communion helps us remember what Jesus did for us. This will keep us from slipping into a place of pride and becoming a sitting duck for the devil.

As I write these words, I've now been out of the mud of drug addiction and alcoholism for over twelve years. Jesus reached in and pulled me out, and now He steadies me daily. I enjoy holding His hand. Walking with Him is what life is all about. Remember, Jesus is the One who is life itself. The mud no longer looks like fun. You don't need dope to cope when you have Christ. Jesus is the way, the truth and the life. (See John 14:6) In His presence is the fullness of joy. You can't get that from a joint, you can't get that from a bottle, and you can't get that from a bag. True peace only comes from the Prince of Peace.

In and out of the mud isn't your destiny. You can be free.

Remembering this will keep you from repeating your mistakes. Remembering what Jesus has done will keep you from repeating behaviors that only lead back to the mud and the mire. You can get out and stay out.

Communion, taken together, regularly, was a part of the DNA of the early church. I believe all the believers were in awe because their eyes were all on Christ through times of communion and worship. They remained focused on Jesus and on the mission He gave them. This changed the way they lived, and they changed the world.

John, if you're still tracking with me, God will bring you out of that barroom and set you free from that unhealthy lifestyle. John, call upon the name of Jesus today. Don't wait another moment. He will save you and set you free. Anyone who calls on the name of the Lord will be saved. Jesus loves you!

THE RESPONSE OF THE RESCUED

The response of someone who has been rescued—saved—is a lifestyle of gratitude.

The writer of Psalm 116 captures the natural and organic thankfulness of someone who's been rescued.

> *"What can I offer the Lord for all he has done for me?"*
> *(Psalm 116:12)*

After crying out for help and being rescued by God, the psalmist is left with a burning desire to give something back to God for setting him free from the ropes of death. (See verse 3.) He is overwhelmed with gratitude for the help and love he has received.

The response of the rescued is an attitude of gratitude that changes the way you live. When God rescues you, when God *saves* you, serving Him is the natural response.

Even rescue scenes in movies capture this truth. Whether it is being rescued from a burning building by a fire fighter or being pulled out from under a smashed vehicle on the highway, the one who is rescued always makes a vow to the rescuer that goes something like this:

Listen! I want to thank you for saving me, you showed up at the right time. I owe you my life. Anything you need, day or night, just call and I'll be there. Anything, and I mean anything, please let me know. Thank you so much. I'm forever indebted to you!

A response is a reaction to something.

- If you are touched by poison, you become itchy.
- If you are rained on, you become wet.
- If you are touched by fire, you become burned.
- If you are touched (or rescued) by God, you become thankful.

The result of being rescued by the hand of God is a burning heart of thankfulness that changes your perspective on life. You now have a desire to live for the One who saved you. The "saved" always have a desire to "serve." You don't need to be talked into serving when you've been saved; you look for opportunities to serve the One who responded to your call for help. Jesus will always be on your lips, not last on your list. This is what love does. Love unseals lips!

Psalm 116:16 will become the drumbeat of your life…

> *"O Lord, I am your servant; yes, I am your servant, born into your household; you have freed me from my chains."*

GUSHING WITH GRATITUDE

In Scripture, when the woman at the well encountered the love of Jesus in John 4, her natural response was to tell others about it. Her testimony brought many others from her village to Jesus. Many came to believe in Jesus because one woman was gushing with gratitude. The love of Jesus unsealed her lips and, immediately, she became an evangelist.

I love the other Samaritans' response…

"Many Samaritans from the village believed in Jesus because the woman had said, "He told me everything I ever did!" When they came out to see him, they begged him to stay in their village. So he stayed for two days, long enough for many more to hear his message and believe. Then they said to the woman, "Now we believe, not just because of what you told us, but because we have heard him ourselves. Now we know that he is indeed the Savior of the world."
(John 4:39–42)

Communion will keep you gushing with gratitude for all that Jesus has done for you. Communion keeps the flames of *first love* alive. When you live this way, others take notice. This is what it means to be a witness. Communion will keep you continually gushing with an attitude of gratitude, to where even your smile will point people to Jesus. One phrase from your lips of love will pull others into a personal encounter with the King. Anointed phrases lead others into His presence. Unpolished words from a raw encounter change lives.

I believe God is raising up a generation of "fire-lip" Christians, and that when they simply share their personal testimony, those hearing it will immediately repent and cry out to the Lord for salvation. This will happen in the grocery store, the bank, the backyard and at the altar. Jesus is ready to pull a coal from the altar in heaven and touch your lips with it. When you've been touched and purified by fire, your words will break people free from the chains of the liar.

As I was walking through our church one day, a little boy from our daycare came to me bursting with excitement, saying, "Hey Travis, I'm going to a waterpark!" He was fired up and looking forward to a weekend of water fun. Kids amaze me. Do you want to know how I know that he was excited to go to the waterpark? Because he told me so.

His excitement led him to share it with me.

The things that excite us are the things we share with others. For a long time, I've been excited every day to share Jesus with others. Waterparks are fun, but right now, the world needs to hear about the *living* water. Refusing to share your faith is robbing someone of the opportunity to find hope. And stealing is still a sin.

I don't know about you, but that fact that God saved me still excites me. My lips are on fire. Life isn't a bummer; it's a gift. God did for me what I could not do for myself—and that fires me up. I would have been dead on a couch if it wasn't for Him. I believe in all my heart that it's impossible to be excited about Jesus and not share Him with others. When you know Him, you can't help but be excited about Him. You will naturally gush with gratitude.

"Let the redeemed of the Lord say so." (Psalm 107:2 NKJV)

I believe that every time the woman at the well took communion throughout her life, she remembered that day at the well. That was the day everything changed. The Source of love showed up in her life so that she could stop looking for love in all the wrong places.

Every time I take communion, I think of that apartment at 200 Shaw Avenue, and of Jesus knocking on the door. I think of Him speaking to me through Revelation 3:20. When I take communion, I remember that I'm a friend of Jesus, and my jaw stays on the floor.

. . .

RESCUED FOR A REASON

> *"For you have rescued me from death; you have kept my feet from slipping. So now I can walk in your presence, O God, in your life-giving light." (Psalm 56:13)*

Jesus rescued us for a reason. He brings us out of darkness and into His marvelous light. He keeps our feet from slipping so we can walk in His presence and shine His life-giving light into the lives of others. He rescues us, restores us, trains us and places us on His rescue team. To be a Christian is to be on God's rescue team. We are the medics of a mighty God.

We are the soldiers of a strong Savior. We are the rescue squad of the Redeemer. The lost, the abandoned, the bound and the broken are waiting for someone to throw them a lifesaver and pull them to Jesus.

If you had a lifesaver, you wouldn't walk by someone who was drowning. You would throw them the lifesaver and pull them to safety.

People are drowning in sin, hopelessness, addiction, fear, deception and depression. When you share your faith, when you shine His life-giving light, you are throwing them a lifesaver. If you walk by, or if you stay silent, *you are letting them drown!*

A WAKEUP CALL

Early one morning, Haven came busting into our bedroom. First, he ran to his mom's side of the bed, got right in her face and shouted, "Rise and shine!" Then, with the same sense of urgency, he ran to my side of the bed, got right in my face and again shouted, "Rise and Shine!" Then he took off down the stairs.

The Holy Spirit immediately brought Isaiah 60 to my mind:

"Arise, shine, for your light has come, and the glory of the Lord rises upon you. See, darkness covers the earth and thick darkness is over the peoples, but the Lord rises upon you and his glory appears over you." (Isaiah 60:1–2 NIV)

Right this moment, I believe God is getting in the face of His kids, His Church, and saying, with great urgency, "Rise and shine!" God is sounding an alarm. Some of His rescue team has fallen asleep. Some of His kids have grown cold with complacency and have become numb to the urgency of the hour. It's not time to run and hide; it's time to rise up as Jesus' rescue team and shine His light in these dark days. It's not time to cower in fear; it's time to share our faith. Stop walking by the drowning people.

If you're reading these words, you were born for such a time as this!

You're alive *now* to shine *now*!

One night, a friend and I hit the streets to bless, encourage and pray with people. As we came around a street corner, we saw flashing police lights. A lady walking her dog came up to us, saying, "You don't want to go down there! Don't go down there!" When I asked why, she didn't say anything but just kept walking. It was kind of weird, but to me and my friend, it just confirmed the direction the Lord wanted us to go, because we are called to run into darkness to be the light.

As we got closer to the flashing lights, we could see it was a vehicular accident. A police officer talking to a young lady in a smashed vehicle. The front end was crunched, and she seemed shaken. One of the witnesses told me she was the driver.

As soon as the officer finished asking her questions, I walked up to her crumpled vehicle, grabbed her shaking hands, and asked if she was hurting and if I could pray for her. She agreed. As she continued to tremble through the lingering shock of the accident, we prayed.

Then I moved out of the way as the police were continuing to do their thing. My friend and I talked with the onlookers about Jesus. We had church, right there at the scene of this accident. The place we had been warned not to go was exactly where we needed to go.

Let me stop and say, Christianity is not about playing it safe and avoiding danger. We were able to sow a lot of seeds that night. If you avoid messy situations, you'll never see a harvest. You can't follow Christ and live a pristine life. If you are pristine, it means you are unused. God led us right where He wanted us that night, and as His kids, we were available to be used by Him.

A few minutes later, a friend of the woman in the accident came to give her a ride home because her vehicle was inoperable. As she sat in her friend's car while the police were continuing their investigation, I received a nudge from the Holy Spirt to talk to her some more.

I went over to her friend's vehicle, reached in and held her hands again. I began to tell her more about Jesus and what He's done in my life. I got to share part of my testimony with her. As soon as I mentioned that I had gotten clean from drugs and alcohol, a well of tears flowed because, wouldn't you know it, she also struggled with addiction. It was part of the reason the accident had occurred. She was under the influence of something.

I knew in that moment that I was right where Jesus needed me to be. This was one of the reasons He rescued me. I got to be His hands, feet and mouthpiece to His daughter in need.

Right then and there, at the scene of an accident, in the middle of her dark night in which she had put herself and others in harm's way, the love of God crashed in on her and she gave Jesus her life. While holding her hands, I led her to the Lord. When she realized that even though she had messed up, it didn't change God's love for her, she naturally surrendered. She was undone. As we said, "Amen," her jaw was on the floor, and so was mine.

A devotion to communion will help you to remember that you were rescued for this very reason.

If you are out in the world rescuing others and serving the One who saved you, satan will never again be able to enslave you.

EXAMINE

As I said at the beginning of this section, communion is a two-sided coin. *Remembrance*, which we just covered, and now the other side: *reflection* or *self-examination*. The apostle Paul shows us this side of the coin:

> *"So then whoever eats the bread or drinks the cup of the Lord in a way that is unworthy [of Him] will be guilty of [profaning and sinning against] the body and blood of the Lord. But a person must [prayerfully] examine himself [and his relationship to Christ], and only when he has done so*

should he eat of the bread and drink of the cup." (1
Corinthians 11:27–28 AMP)

While meditating on communion and being still before the Lord, I went into a vision. I saw a helicopter pilot preparing to take off. He was concerned about his fuel level, wondering if he would have enough to get to his destination. He decided to take the journey on the partial tank of fuel anyway. Part way through his flight, he hit something that caused a great deal of exterior damage to the one side of the helicopter. Now, with exterior damage and the fuel level getting lower, the pilot became alarmed. This damage caused him to realize his desperate need to turn back, fix the damage, and fill up on fuel.

Communion is a check-up like that, a time of reflection and self-examination.

In this vision, I believe the Lord was showing me that the damage came because the fuel was low. When things get low on fuel, your engine spits, sputters, and begin to lose power. The function of a helicopter is dependent on fuel. You can't fly without it. If the pilot would have filled up before flying, he might have made it to his destination without inflicting damage and enduring the costly repairs.

The pilot's neglect was the reason for the damage.

Never take communion merely because everyone else is doing it! That's dangerous. Communion is a time for remembrance and self-examination. It's a time to slow down from the busyness of life, a time to check your heart in the light of God's love, so you don't find yourself flying through life with a low love-tank.

Communion, when not done religiously, can keep you from unnecessary damage. It can keep bitterness from growing into resentment. It can keep a lustful thought from turning into an affair. It can keep you moving forward and into your destiny on a full tank of God's love.

The church in Corinth turned communion into a selfish party and weren't allowing the Holy Spirit to examine their hearts. Check out this definition for the word *examine:*

Examine: to see whether a thing is genuine or not. (See 2 Corinthians 13:5.)

If we skip the self-examination side of the communion coin, we will slip into counterfeit Christianity. Fake faith helps no one and hurts everyone. We must allow the Holy Spirit to search us. *Souls are at stake*, and the last thing the world needs is more fakeness.

Communion, again, is a time for self-examination. If we are regularly examining ourselves—our thoughts, attitudes, and behaviors—we will catch things before we fall.

People go to the doctor for regular checkups and to prevent sicknesses or tumors from growing and getting worse. If we go to Jesus for regular checkups, we will prevent sin before it becomes fully grown and leads to death. (See James 1:14.)

No one just falls into sin. Falling back into sin—ending up back in Egypt—happens when we forget Jesus and neglect self-examination. Self-examination requires self-honesty.

- When was the last time you had a checkup with Jesus?
- Are you keeping secrets?
- Are you minimizing and justifying behaviors that are less than God's best for you?

- Are you living a double life? Are you behaving one way at church and another way at home, at work, or out with friends?
- Do you only take communion because everyone else is doing it?

If communion is merely a religious ritual, it could be detrimental to your life. Just as people go to the doctor for yearly checkups and physical examinations, communion is a *spiritual physical*. Its benefits are wholeness and freedom. Regular checkups help to prevent your health from regressing. Communion helps to keep you moving forward in spiritual growth and in fulfilling the assignment Jesus has for you. Communion helps you to remain genuine.

Paul said that sickness, weakness, and death are the result of skipping this side of the communion coin. (See 1 Corinthians 11:30.)

Religious rituals without a real relationship with Jesus can kill you. Check-box Christianity is a cancer. Communion is serious.

Don't take communion without a time of reflection and self-examination. If there's been wrong in your life, make it right. If there is sin in your life, confess it. If there are secrets in your life, bring them into the light.

You don't have to be a helicopter with unnecessary damage. You can fulfill your God-given destiny and be with Him for all eternity.

UNBOX YOUR FREEDOM

"He is so rich in kindness and grace that he purchased our

freedom with the blood of his Son and forgave our sins."
(Ephesians 1:7)

As a parent, I've never bought Haven a toy and said, "You are to keep this in its box and only look at it." My wife and I don't buy toys for him to look at and not enjoy. Toys are to be enjoyed and played with. I like it when Haven enjoys what his mother and I work hard to pay for. The reward of hard work is seeing the joy it brings to others.

Hebrews 12:2, speaking of Jesus, says, *"For the joy set before him he endured the cross"* (NIV).

The joy set before Jesus included addicts getting clean and becoming productive members of society. The joy set before Him included the hopeless finding hope. The joy set before Him included you being able to forgive those who have harmed you. The joy set before Him included children getting their moms and dads back. The joy set before Him included parents getting their children back. The joy set before Him included people no longer living to please only themselves. The joy set before Him included His kids being unified and working together for good. The joy set before Him included destroying the works of the devil. The joy set before Him included no longer ever being separated from *you.*

Jesus came to earth and went to the cross—*for you!* You were the joy set before Him.

Jesus came to earth and paid the price on the cross for our freedom, not so we would keep it in a box for later but so that we would open it and enjoy it now. Salvation is a free gift to be enjoyed *now*, not some day when we get to heaven. It delights God's heart when we enjoy what He paid for with His precious blood. A devotion to communion will help you to remember the free gift of salvation that is meant to change your life, now and forevermore.

It's time to unbox your freedom and walk in what was fully, not partially, purchased. Taking communion helps you to remember what Jesus did for you on the cross. Let's cherish this truth of freedom.

This was also the burden on the heart of the apostle Paul. Check out his words to the church in Galatia:

> *"Let me be clear, the Anointed One has set us free—not partially, but completely and wonderfully free! We must always cherish this truth and stubbornly refuse to go back into the bondage of our past." (Galatians 5:1 TPT)*

Our freedom is the reward of His suffering. Sin no longer having dominion over you is the reward of His suffering. Healing and deliverance are the reward of His suffering. You becoming a new creation is the reward of His suffering.

He paid for our freedom so we could access it and enjoy it—*now!*

We are not called to crawl our way to heaven while the enemy daily kicks our butts. We don't just remain a sinner saved by grace. Through Christ, we become more than conquerors, people who live by faith. Sons and daughters of the King live differently. We are called to live as citizens of heaven. We are called to destroy of the works of darkness, not to get run over by works of darkness.

Jesus paid my debt on the cross with His broken body and blood. I don't know about you, but I want Jesus to receive His full reward for the blood He poured out for my sin. I want Peter's revelation burning in my heart, 24/7. Check this out:

> *"He personally carried our sins in his body on the cross so that we can be dead to sin and live for what is right. By his wounds you are healed. Once you were like sheep who wandered away. But now you have turned to your Shepherd, the Guardian of your souls." (1 Peter 2:24–25)*

The cross must be personal to you. Don't leave your freedom in a box! Remember the blood! You don't have to wander in the wilderness of your past anymore. You don't have to go back to bondage.

The flesh, the sinful nature, is not—I repeat, *is not*—more powerful than the blood of Jesus. If Jesus is your Master, sin can't be.

When we remember what He's done for us, lies have a hard time creeping into our lives. That is why communion is so important.

Let's look at Jesus' words from the Last Supper again:

> *"This cup is the new covenant between God and his people —an agreement confirmed with my blood, which is poured out as a sacrifice for you." (Luke 22:20)*

We're robbed of blood-bought freedom when we forget the blood. Forgetting the blood is the birthplace of backsliding and relapse. Remembering it is the foundation of a life of unlimited freedom and joy. The cross made it possible for us to leave our pasts behind. The resurrection makes it possible for us to enter the promised land. Pentecost provides the power of the Holy Spirit, that we might walk in victory and show others the way.

When you remember the blood that paid for your sins, and the new covenant that Jesus inaugurated, you remember that you are forgiven and deeply loved. When you remember how much He loves you, loneliness can no longer imprison you and the enemy's lies will no longer hold you hostage.

When I remember Him, I don't want to sin!

Sinning is the last thing on my mind when my eyes are fixed on Jesus. Don't keep this gift wrapped up and in a box. Enjoy it now! Enjoy Him now!

Make remembering Jesus a high priority. Remain devoted to communion, to both sides of its coin.

4

SECTION 4: DEVOTION TO PRAYER

"Unless I had the spirit of prayer, I could do nothing."
—Charles Finney

The fourth component in the awe factor is a devotion to prayer. We should never get over this next statement: We were created to communicate with our Creator.

God—who spoke the stars into existence, who knows your name and the number of hairs on your head, who knit you together in your mother's womb, whose thoughts for you outnumber the grains of sand on all the beaches in the world —wants to hear from you and talk with you. You matter to God! You were made to marvel!

I begin this section with those words because reverence for God is the foundation of communication with Him. Prayer is holy. Those who have a hard time *hearing* from the Lord have stopped *revering* the Lord. Whenever there is a hearing issue, there's usually a reverence issue. Reverence is being in awe. Reverence is deep love and respect. Reverence brings an *attentiveness* to God's voice because there's *respect* for His voice. I believe the reason some hear from the Lord and others don't is simply this: some *want to* and others *don't*; some *respect Him* and others *don't*.

Not taking time to pray, worship and study the Word shows a disrespect for God. Anyone who continues to disrespect God doesn't really know Him. When you truly know Him, you adore Him and prayer excites you.

Prayer is one of the primary ways we grow in the knowledge of God. Jesus said, *"My sheep hear My voice"* (John 10:27 NASB).

You can hear from Jesus and talk to Jesus, if you *want* to. I started talking to Jesus when I was a child because I was taught a simple prayer.

NEVER UNDERESTIMATE THE POWER OF A SIMPLE PRAYER

Maybe you were taught this prayer too:

Now I lay me down to go to sleep,

I pray the Lord my soul to keep;

If I should die before I 'wake,

I pray the Lord my soul to take.

This prayer was my introduction to *prayer*. I remember learning this prayer as a little kid and saying it often before bedtime. While this prayer didn't get me living on fire for Jesus, reading the Bible, going to church or worshiping the Lord, it did teach me that I could talk to God. Learning this prayer planted a powerful seed in my life that, I realize now, was never uprooted. The enemy, in all his attacks against me, was unable to get his hands on this seed of prayer. Prayer is that powerful. We must never underestimate the power of a simple prayer.

Fast forward many years later to my life as a drug addict. I hated myself and was sick and tired of being a slave to drugs and alcohol, but I couldn't stop using. There were many nights and early mornings when I was so strung out on cocaine that I couldn't sleep. I would roll around in bed, tossing and turning, but no rest came. Peace of mind seemed so far away. I would lay in bed for hours, my mind racing a hundred miles an hour, obsessively wondering why I couldn't fall asleep.

In the middle of this mental chaos and frustration, this thought would come breaking in like beams of sunlight through dark storm clouds: *It's because I haven't prayed yet.* Notice, I wasn't thinking, *It's because I'm high on cocaine and living in sin.* No joking, I would then begin to pray, for sleep but also for others. And wouldn't you know it, I was able to fall asleep.

After I got clean, the Lord showed me that during those restless nights, what I had heard was Him speaking to me. That thought was His voice. As I pondered this, the Lord revealed to me what He was saying: "Travis, even though you were a hot mess then, I still wanted to be the last person you talked to before you went to bed." He wanted me to know that He is the God who gives rest to the weary. He wanted me to know that even in the midst of struggle, He still wants to be there for me.

> *"Then Jesus said, 'Come to me, all of you who are weary and carry heavy burdens, and I will give you rest.'"*
> *(Matthew 11:28)*

I believe that because I was taught "As I Lay Me Down to Sleep" when I was young, the Holy Spirit was able to use it as a reminder of the importance of prayer as I grew older. That blows me away. Even though I wasn't living for God, He still loved me and wanted to hear from me. Looking back on it now, I clearly see God's mighty hand at work throughout my life. He was trying to get my attention my entire life. That's amazing!

Teaching kids simple prayers when they are young will anchor them to a life of prayer as they grow older. We must never underestimate the power of a simple prayer.

TO THE PARENTS, FAMILY, AND FRIENDS OF PRODIGALS

I record a weekly video called *Monday Marvels* to help people start each week with their eyes on Jesus. I don't believe you have to experience "the Mondays" when every day is a gift from God. In the videos, I share Scriptures, testimonies, and prophetic words to encourage people.

While filming a few videos at a local park with my brother Aaron, who does all the camera work, we sparked a conversation with two women who came walking by us as we were packing up our equipment.

I asked, "Hey, how are you doing this evening?"

They replied, "We're doing good. Just out for a walk." Then they asked, "How are you guys doing?"

We responded, "We are doing amazing. We're making videos for Jesus."

Drop the J-Bomb!

They replied, "Awesome! We're on the Jesus team as well."

We continued making some small talk, and as they were about to leave, I introduced myself, "My name is Travis Habbershon. It was so good to meet you. Have a great evening."

One of the women paused for a moment and then, with a surprised look on her face, said, "Travis Habbershon? Your name is Travis Habbbershon? You're a local pastor, right?"

"Yes," I told her.

Then, with joy in her eyes, she said, "I have prayer journals at home with your name in it."

I was in awestruck.

For many years during my addiction, I worked at a chocolate factory—and yes, it was pretty sweet! That was where I was working in 2007 when I left work to try to kill myself. I worked there on an off during the darkest parts of my addiction.

Prior to my suicide attempt, one of my coworkers around that time was an on-fire follower of Jesus. He would try to talk to me about the Lord and showed me great kindness, even though I didn't care to hear it. Even though my heart was hard, he offered me rides when I needed them and reached out and encouraged me with the love of Jesus. He was unashamed of the gospel. (See Romans 1:16.)

What I didn't know at that time was that he was going to a small group Bible study. Every time he went, and they asked for prayer requests, he would say, "Pray for Travis Habbershon."

And there we were at a park, making videos for Jesus some twelve or thirteen years later, and by divine appoint, I met one of my intercessors I didn't even know I had. She got to see the fruit of her labor of love.

I told her how grateful I was for the faithful prayers of both her and the group, even though they didn't hear of any breakthrough right away. And then, wouldn't you know it, I got to pray for her. It was such a beautiful moment.

Think about this with me. Because we said "Hi" to a couple of women walking in the park, I got to see that it was the power of intercessory prayer that helped me to break out of the pain and misery of drug addiction. It was the seeds of love sowed by my coworker and several intercessory prayer warriors that helped to bring me out of darkness and into the light.

My jaw is still on the floor. I'm a product of intercessory prayer. They prayed me through to freedom. Intercessory prayer is simply praying on behalf of another person.

They were spiritual snipers in my life, interceding for my salvation and deliverance. I believe, with all my heart, that I heard that knock on my door because their prayers went to war against the darkness and the demons that were trying to destroy me.

I would also like to add that it was that same on-fire coworker who gave me the Bible I opened up when I had my life-changing encounter with Jesus through Revelation 3:20. Every prayer we pray, every seed we plant, matters!

I share all of this to say that if you have kids or loved ones who have walked away from their faith in Christ, and you taught them simple prayers when they were children, take comfort in knowing that those seeds are still there. What the enemy can't uproot, he'll try to cover over and bury with lies. Please, never stop praying for them, even when it looks as though nothing is happening. We walk by faith, not by sight. Persist in prayer, just as that small group did for me. Keep planting seeds and refuse to believe the lies of the enemy.

Keep praying for the memory of those seeds of prayer to surface in their minds again. Pray that the Spirit of truth would break through the lies, and, just as the memory of his father's house brought the prodigal son home in Luke 15, we too will see more prodigal sons and daughters come out of the pig pens of this world and reunite with Jesus through the power of intercession.

PRAYER:

> Father, in the name of Jesus, bring (insert your loved one's name) home through the memories and seeds of prayer that were planted in their life. Rain down fresh water on every seed of prayer and reawaken their desire and need for You. In Jesus' name we pray. Amen!

DOLPHINS AND A SAND DOLLAR

While my wife and I were on our honeymoon in 2013, I had a life-changing encounter with God that revolutionized my personal prayer life.

For our honeymoon, we went to Myrtle Beach, South Carolina. It was the first time I had ever been there. One day, we took a stroll up the beach to search for some seashells, and spent time enjoying God's beautiful creation. As we walked along the beach, my wife kept finding these amazing shells, and every so often, she would find broken pieces of sand dollars.

I had never seen a sand dollar before. These broken pieces fascinated me. All of God's creations reveal His glory.

Moses became so fascinated by God that he cried out, *"Show me your glory"* (Exodus 33:18 NIV). As my wife was finding all these sea treasures, I prayed a similar prayer to the one Moses prayed. I said to God, "Show me something amazing!" Remember, we must never underestimate the power of a simple prayer.

In that five-word prayer, my heart's desire was to find a whole sand dollar. The broken pieces were cool, but I wanted to find one without a chip or a crack. Not long after my prayer, I looked to my right, about forty yards or so into the ocean, and I saw dolphins jumping and swimming. It was amazing. I like to tell people that I swam with the dolphins because my feet were in the water when I saw them. That was also a first for me. I had never seen dolphins swimming in their natural habitat before. I was blown away. God heard my prayer.

In that moment, my gratitude to God for His goodness and faithfulness went to a whole new level. He was teaching me more about prayer, and the best was yet to come.

We walked down to a pier and then decided to turn around and head back to our vehicle. I was getting a gnarly sunburn by that point. Still awestruck by the dolphins, I walked in the sand as the ocean tide washed over my feet. Then, as I was watching the tide wash over my feet, out of the corner of my eye I saw a round object riding in on the water, being delivered like a gift and landing right in front of me.

Mesmerized, I reached down and, wouldn't you know it, it was a completely whole sand dollar. I grabbed it, held it up in the air, and yelled, in childlike wonder, "Look, honey! I got a whole one!"

I was *undone*. God showed me His glory. It's not like hundreds of sand dollars were washing up on the beach at that time. This was the only whole one we saw on a several-hour-long walk on the beach, and it was delivered right at my feet. The timing of my walking and this sand dollar catching the right wave at the right moment could only be orchestrated by the Creator.

Prayer is so personal, and in that moment, I really felt like a friend to God. Christianity is way more than a service one day a week. It's about friendship and intimacy with the Creator of dolphins and sand dollars. Prayer isn't just something we do when we're in pain or in trouble. It's more than that. Prayer is also the platform God uses to do things, simply because He likes to make us smile.

You need to know that God really does love you. He likes to make you smile. He enjoys blowing your mind.

This would be a cool story if it ended there, but it didn't. Jesus isn't shy. He wants to reveal Himself to each of us in personal and jaw-dropping ways. He loves to put His signature on the encounter.

After we got home from our honeymoon, I couldn't shake the memory of the sand dollar. I pondered that precious moment a lot. One Sunday after church, the Holy Spirit spoke these words to me: "Look up the sand dollar."

So, I typed in "sand dollar" into a search engine and this phrase popped up and jumped off the screen: "Legend of the Sand Dollar." My first thought was, *Whoa! There's a legend of the sand dollar!* With great curiosity and excitement, I clicked on it, and this poem came up:

There's a lovely little legend that I would like to tell,
Of the birth and death of Jesus, found in this lowly shell.
If you examine closely, you'll see that you find here,
Four nail holes and a fifth one, made by a Roman's spear.
On one side the Easter lily, its center is the star,
That appeared unto the shepherds and led them from afar.
The Christmas Poinsettia etched on the other side,
Reminds us of His birthday, our happy Christmastide.
Now break the center open, and here you will release,
The five white doves awaiting, to spread Good Will and
Peace.
This simple little symbol, Christ left for you and me,
To help us spread His Gospel, through all Eternity.

— AUTHOR UNKNOWN

It said the author is unknown, but I know the author. He's the Author of life, Jesus Christ, and He loves to blow our minds. I was undone when I picked up the sand dollar, but after I read the poem, I knew my prayer life would never be the same. Jesus delights in revealing Himself to us.

A devotion to prayer isn't tough to have when you're burning with His love.

Again, prayer isn't something we do only when we're in trouble or need help; it's a conversation between friends.

TENT TIME

Moses, the one who cried, *"Show me your glory,"* had tent-time with God. Tent-time is needed for a growing prayer life.

One day, I made a tent out of a blanket on our couch for Haven and I to play under. One thing I'm learning as a father is that it's not always an expensive toy that brings a child joy. Parents, we can be creative. Haven and I had a blast with a blanket and our imagination.

We played for a while, and as I was leaving the tent, he said to me, "Dad, I want you to stay with me!"

In the tent, we were face to face, no one else, just father and son. As my son's words melted my heart again, the Holy Spirit reminded me of Moses' relationship with God.

Check out these verses:

> *"It was Moses' practice to take the Tent of Meeting and set it up some distance from the camp. Everyone who wanted to make a request of the Lord would go to the Tent of Meeting outside the camp. ...Inside the Tent of Meeting, the Lord would speak to Moses face to face, as one speaks to a friend."* *(Exodus 33:7)*

The *"Tent of Meeting"* was a place to talk to God. We all need a tent (a place) where we can talk to the Lord. Friends of God have tent meetings with God.

NO TENT-TIME WITH GOD = NO FRIENDSHIP WITH GOD

It's important to have time when you distance yourself from others and be alone with your heavenly Father. The Tent of Meeting was set up some distance from the camp.

Jesus taught this same truth. He said, *"But when you pray, go away by yourself, shut the door behind you, and pray to your*

Father in private. Then your Father, who sees everything, will reward you" (Matthew 6:6)

I love how God provides reminders through my son of His desire for a personal relationship with me. The tent blanket was cool, but what made it special was that it provided a close space for a father and son to be together. Tent-time will strengthen your prayer life because the tent shuts out distractions. Distance from noise makes it easier to hear God's voice. Prayer is about talking and listening.

It's important to know that tent-time can take place anywhere—a prayer closet, your bedroom or in in nature. Find a place free of distractions that works for you. Then, when Jesus says, "Stay with Me," you should *stay* a little longer.

Tent-meeting-makers experience His glory.

Moses went directly to the source and became friends with God. Because of Jesus, we can do the same.

GET IN THE SINK AND DRINK

> *"The Lord will guide you continually, giving you water when you are dry and restoring your strength. You will be like a well-watered garden, like an ever-flowing spring."*
> *(Isaiah 58:11)*

While having breakfast with Kelsey one morning, Gemma, our cat, jumped up and into our sink, as she often does, and began licking drops of water coming out of the spout. Kelsey made a joking comment, "Gemma likes to go right to the source."

As I pondered her comment, the Holy Spirit gave illumination to her words. Even with a saucer full of water on the floor, Gemma went to the source. She chose *source* over *saucer*.

Here's what the Lord spoke to me: "Never settle for sips from a saucer when you can go right to the source."

- Are you settling for sips from a saucer when the source is calling you?
- Are you going to church on Sunday but not praying by yourself on Monday?
- Are you listening to sermons but never opening your Bible?

Saucer-sippers live depleted and get defeated, but those who find the source live fully and win the fight. Saucer-sippers barely make it from Sunday to Sunday because they never actually go to the source. It's time to get in the sink and drink, every day. Tent-time is sink-time.

A personal prayer life keeps you like a well-watered garden and restores your strength. Don't depend on others to feed you. You can receive the Bread of Life right from the Baker Himself. Don't depend on mere sips from others. Get in the sink and drink your fill from the source.

The fruit of tent-time is transformation. Going right to the source is the key to growing in intimacy with the Lord. A good sermon will lead you to the sink. Talking with other believers about Jesus creates a hunger for tent-time with Jesus.

We need time with others, and we also need tent-time with the Lord.

Here are some verses to meditate on...

> *"You are my refuge and my shield; your word is my **source** of hope."* (Psalm 119:114, emphasis added)

> *"I pray that God, the **source** of hope, will fill you completely with joy and peace because you trust in him. Then you will overflow with confident hope through the power of the Holy Spirit."* (Romans 15:13, emphasis added)

> *"There I will go to the altar of God, to God—the **source** of all my joy. I will praise you with my harp, O God, my God!"* (Psalm 43:4, emphasis added)

> *"All praise to God, the Father of our Lord Jesus Christ. God is our merciful Father and the **source** of all comfort."* (2 Corinthians 1:3, emphasis added)

> *"In this way, God qualified [Jesus] as a perfect High Priest, and he became the **source** of eternal salvation for all those who obey him."* (Hebrews 5:9, emphasis added)

THE GREATEST NEED OF THE HOUR

While listening to my pastor preach one Sunday morning in 2020, he began to share about how the apostle John laid his head on Jesus' chest and heard the very heartbeat of God. (See John 13:25.)

When he made that statement, the alarm from the firehouse up the street began going off. It was as if those very words triggered the alarm. I felt the Lord saying to me, with great urgency, "The lack of intimacy with Me is now an emergency in the church."

After I got home, the Lord took me to Jeremiah. The Holy Spirit brought these words to mind as I pondered the meaning of the alarm: *"My people...do not know me."*

God is sounding a Jeremiah 4:22-alarm right now:

> *"My people are fools; they do not know me. They are senseless children; they have no understanding. They are skilled in doing evil; they know not how to do good." (Jeremiah 4:22 NIV)*

Without a prayer life, it is impossible to get to know the Lord. When you know the God of Wonders, you will live a life of awe and wonder. You were made to marvel.

It's sad but most people would rather scroll through a screen than search through the Scriptures and grow in the knowledge of God. Trash is the new treasure. Our world is more fascinated with TV and video games than the glory of God revealed in Christ Jesus. People are more passionate about politics than prayer and the presence of God. Many go to church on Sunday, but their minds are more focused on leaving so they don't miss a minute of a football game. They have no desire to be a doer of the word; they only want to check their religious box.

Hardened hearts and desert-dry eyes are the plague of the day. Being tearless reveals our lack of nearness to the heart of Jesus.

This is an emergency in the heart of God. Emergencies require immediate action. It's time to reprioritize our lives with prayer as the foundation, or else we are headed for disaster. It doesn't end well for those who don't *know* God. (See Matthew 7:21–23.)

Sometimes, we need to be reminded of our heavenly Father's heart and desire. Meditate on these three passages until a fire for prayer ignites in your spirit.

> *1. [The Lord says,] "I looked forward to your calling me 'Father,' and I wanted you never to turn from me" (Jeremiah 3:19).*

God looks forward to you calling Him "Dad," so you can be together forever. Every father knows the joy and excitement of hearing your child say "Dada!" for the first time. The Lord loves to hear from you. Our heavenly Father sent His Son to die so there could be a day when you would say His name. Every time I read that passage in Jeremiah, I can't help but think of Jesus' prayer in John 17.

> *2. "Father, I desire that they also whom You gave Me may be with Me where I am, that they may behold My glory which You have given Me; for You loved Me before the foundation of the world" (John 17:24 NKJV).*

Jesus desires intimacy. He wants you to be with Him now and forevermore. When Jesus was knocking on the door of the church in Revelation 3, an alarm was going off. This verse is one of my life verses and extremely personal to me, as I mentioned in Section 1. Now let us dive a little deeper into it.

> *3. "Behold, I stand at the door and knock. If anyone hears My voice and opens the door, I will come in to him and dine with him, and he with Me" (Revelation 3:20 NKJV).*

Whenever there is distance between His heart and our heart, there will be an alarm sounding. Jesus wants nearness. He can't stand distance because He knows that's when we get into danger. Distance leads to danger. Jesus shed His precious blood on the cross for *dining* not for *distance*.

Jesus' knocking (the alarm) reveals our need for Him, but also His desire to dine with us. He knocks because *we need*, but also because *He wants*. He stands at the door hoping someone will hear his knock and let Him in. He knocks for individuals who need to be *saved* but also for His churches that need to be *revived*.

Intimacy is the greatest need of the hour. Only a fool would ignore an alarm. Jesus wants to dine with you forever.

A devotion to prayer helps you hear the alarm when it first goes off. That is why a daily prayer life is important. Responding to the alarm immediately prevents danger. If you keep hitting snooze, your heart will drift further and further from the Lord. This is a danger zone. The enemy prowls around, looking for believers to disconnect from prayer. If you ignore the alarm, you will be pounced upon. Intimacy shouldn't be an option.

Will you respond to the alarm?

If you are constantly being pounced upon, you'll never be aligned with your personal assignment. Your purpose is often revealed and confirmed in prayer. Protect your prayer life!

PRAYER ALIGNS YOU WITH YOUR ASSIGNMENT

A couple of years ago, I was invited to a prayer meeting. This prayer group was focused on praying for our community and for revival to occur. While at the prayer meeting, after a time of worship and intercession, a woman read a *prophetic word* that had been received about our town in 2007. As soon as I heard the *year* the word was received, my spiritual ears opened. When I heard it read, I knew in my spirit that a torch was being passed to me. Remember, it was in 2007 that Jesus knocked on my door.

Here's the prophetic word the woman read:

Lewistown has always been a place where I felt an element of deep sadness and despair. Each time I have driven into town, I felt the weight of this darkness, as well as a strong desire to quickly get out of town to "shake It off."

But on this unique day, something new and refreshing happened. As I drove into town, the sky opened. The sun was so bright, the town seemed unrecognizable. The housetops were illuminated. The town looked like a new place. Something that seemed heavy had lifted and was gone.

I felt the Lord say to me, "See? I will do a new thing here. No longer will this be a place of sadness and despair. Instead, it will be a place filled with My glory—a place of wholeness, healing, salvation and deliverance. People will know it and will travel from miles around to experience the unconditional love found in this place. They will seek salvation, healing and deliverance. Lewistown is a people who have known hardship, sorrow and brokenness. They will be filled with all that *I AM*, for *I AM* love, their Rock, their sure foundation. No one who seeks and trusts in Me will ever be disappointed."

May the God of Isaac, Abraham and Jacob be glorified in this word.

When a torch is passed, there is a transfer of responsibility. This prophetic word aligned me with my heavenly assignment. Prophetic words give clarity and focus to your marching orders. When the torch was passed, I felt the weight of the responsibility, and the excitement of seeing God's heart and plan for our community. Lewistown is where I was born and raised, and where I still live to this very day.

The same year Jesus knocked on my door, this word came forth. Coincidence? I think not. Prayer helps reveal your prophetic timeline. Since I surrendered my life to Jesus, I have found healing, salvation and deliverance. Jesus has done a new thing in me. Each and every day is growing me more and more toward wholeness. God really does make all things new. Communal transformation is the fruit of personal transformation.

A couple of weeks ago, the Lord told me that the key to taking a town for the kingdom of God, taking back any territory from the enemy, is to take "the talk of the town." When something is "the talk of the town," it's what everyone is talking about.

What you say about your community matters. Your conversations at the restaurant, the barber shop, and the grocery store matter. If you walk around saying, "I hate my town; nothing good ever happens here," you are partnering with the enemy and spreading darkness and negativity into the lives of others. Your words are blinding you from seeing beauty, and the more you speak them, the more deceived and negative you become.

When you talk that way, and people see you as a Christian, your words are keeping others from Jesus. *If that's the case, whose team are you on?*

You can wear a Christian T-shirt and still be a captain on the enemy's team. This truth came to me through meditating on this passage:

> *"The whole city celebrates when the godly succeed; they*
> *shout for joy when the wicked die. Upright citizens are good*
> *for a city and make it prosper, but the talk of the wicked*
> *tears it apart." (Proverbs 11:10–11)*

If the talk of the wicked can tear apart a city, what do you think the talk of the righteous can do?

God changes the atmosphere of a city or town by first changing a life. God loves to take *the menaces of society* and turn them into *walking miracles of His glory*. The ripple effect of your life in Christ can push back the powers of hell. Testimonies of a changed life spread hope throughout families and communities, and wage war against the darkness.

When lives are changed, "the talk of the town" changes from negative to positive. Testimonies of the power of God are about to take over your town. Testimonies cause kingdom takeover. There's more good news than bad news. Get ready for head-turning testimonies that shift conversations in every aspect of your community.

When ex-drug addicts become preachers, the talk of the town changes. When families are restored, the talk of the town changes. When marriages are healed, the talk of the town changes. When miracles break out, the talk of the town changes. When churches are more packed than bars, the talk of the town changes. When the blind see, the deaf hear and the lame walk, the city celebrates and the talk of the town changes.

Watch your words and watch your talk. Your talk reveals whose team you're on.

A prayer meeting aligned me with my personal assignment. Prayer places you where God wants you to be. Stay devoted to prayer, friends, and you will stay in alignment with your assignment.

YOUR JAW BELONGS ON THE FLOOR

On a hot and sticky August evening in 2018, I was heading to our church to help a couple restore their marriage. On the way there, I stopped at Dunkin' Donuts to get an iced coffee. When I got out of my truck, I saw a gentleman sitting on a ledge all alone.

I don't know about you but when I see someone alone, I like to check in and make sure they're okay. It's good to talk to people. Remember, a simple "Hello" can be life changing.

I sparked up a conversation with the guy and asked him how he was doing. He told me he was waiting on a taxi. Then he told me he was eating at the restaurant across the street, and that he lives alone and likes to get out when he can.

This led to me to share about the dangers of isolation and the importance of community. Then we talked about Jesus.

He shared his testimony of faith with me and we prayed for a friend of his who was battling cancer, as well as some health issues he was personally facing. We had church right outside Dunkin' Donuts. It was beautiful. I could tell by the smile on his face that he was grateful for the conversation and the prayers.

We said our goodbyes and I went to get my iced coffee.

When I came out, the Holy Spirit gave me a nudge to go back and see if I could give the man a ride. I felt like the Lord wasn't done yet. And besides, with how busy our local taxi service gets, the man may have been waiting for a while. So, I asked him if I could give him a ride.

He jumped in my truck and we headed toward Puff and Snuff, a tobacco shop *at his request*. During our ride there and into Lewistown, we talked about Jesus and he shared a few testimonies with me. Then he said, "When you get to this second traffic light up here, you're going to take a left turn. Then, a couple blocks down, my apartment is on the corner."

About a block before I took the left turn, he said, "When I first moved into this place, I heard that it had been a store-front many years ago, and that the owner committed suicide in the place." He went on to say that when he first started staying there, there seemed to be a darkness present. Then he asked me if I believed in things like that.

I said, "Yes, I do," but then I told him that as a child of God, you can command that stuff to go away in Jesus' name.

He said, "That's exactly what I did!"

I said, "Amen!"

Then, as I took the left turn, it hit me: I knew I was driving him to 200 Shaw Avenue, the place where Jesus found me thirteen years prior.

My jaw was on the floor. I was speechless.

As I pulled in front of the apartment, I was trembling in awe and reverence of God. I asked the man if I could pray for him one more time. He said he was cool with that. We prayed, he thanked me for the ride and got out of my truck. I was so undone, I couldn't even get the words out to tell him in that moment. Plus, I had to get to the counseling meeting with that couple.

I don't know how good my counseling was that night because all I did was tell them the Dunkin' Donuts story and gush with gratitude over how awesome our God is.

Here's the crazy part: about two months before this, I told Kelsey I was feeling a stirring from the Lord to do a video of my testimony from the door of 200 Shaw Avenue. Two months after I said those words, I met the man who was living there, outside of Dunkin' Donuts. Our God is awesome. I believe that most believers miss moments like this because they never say "Hello" to people.

When you live beyond yourself, you'll find yourself in the will of God, and the will of God is a life of awe and wonder. If your faith is boring, you are not following Jesus. Jesus doesn't write boring stories.

Two days later, I went back to 200 Shaw Avenue. Now I was the one knocking on the door. When the man answered, I said, "Hey, buddy. I want you to know that the Lord had a whole lot more in store for us than me just giving you a ride the other day."

He smiled and welcomed me in. As I crossed the threshold, the first thing I noticed was pictures of Jesus all over his walls. The place that had been a nightmare for me was now a place where the presence of God dwelt. What once was hell was now holy ground. We sat down to talk at his kitchen table. It was the same table I had used to shoot heroin, chop up pills and cook crack. Now, I sat there and told this man how Jesus had rescued me in that very place. I shared my testimony with him and we prayed.

It was a full-circle moment.

A couple of months later, my new friend was kneeling beside his bed in prayer when he leaned over and went to be with the Lord. When the paramedics found him bent over beside his bed, they assumed that he had fallen. When his daughters showed up, however, they said, "No, he didn't fall. That's where our dad prayed."

He went on to be with Jesus in prayer at 200 Shaw Avenue. Over coffee with his daughters, I got to hear his story. His name was Ted.

> *"You are the God of great wonders! You demonstrate your awesome power among the nations." (Psalm 77:14)*

I believe that meeting me outside Dunkin' Donuts was one of Ted's last assignments from the Lord before being called home. Meeting me was part of him finishing his race. I'm so grateful for the Holy Spirt, who nudges us because He loves us, and doesn't want us to miss those holy moments.

Reader, you don't have to miss those moments.

When it comes to developing a devotion to prayer. We all need a beginning. If prayer is new to you, simply start by talking to Jesus. Say His name. Share your heart with Him. He loves your voice. Just as communication grows over time in all your earthly relationships, your prayer life will continue to grow as well. Make a beginning and stick with it.

Stay devoted to the teachings of Jesus, to fellowship with other believers and to times of communion and prayer. If you do, your jaw will stay on the floor.

You were made to marvel!

You can remain in awe, my friends. God Bless!

The end.

SMALL GROUP GUIDE

SECTION #1 – DEVOTION TO TEACHING

- *What spoke to you the most in this section?*
- *Is there anything you need to turn away from?*
- *Has your devotion shifted to something other than Jesus?*
- *Have you had a "Big Reveal"?* (share it with your group, don't get stuck on the word "Big" tell your Jesus story)
- *Has the Bible become alive to you?*
- *When is the last time you cried out "HOLD ME DAD!"?*

SECTION #2 – DEVOTION TO FELLOWSHIP

- *What spoke to you the most in this section?*
- *Do you ever struggle with spending too much time in front of a screen?*
- *Share about a time a friend helped you face a fear...*
- *How have others helped you draw closer to Jesus?*
- *Have you ever shared your faith with someone?* (talk about the experience)

- *Who told you about Jesus?*

SECTION #3 – DEVOTION TO COMMUNION

- *What spoke to you the most in this section?*
- *Are you stuck in any unhealthy sin cycles? (don't let shame keep you silent)*
- *What does the cross mean to you?*
- *How has remembering what Jesus did for you changed your life?*
- *How important is reflection and self-examination?*

TAKE COMMUNION! (DON'T RUSH)

first: *take some time to remember Jesus and what He did on the cross. Remember His passionate love for you. Have a time of worship and praise as you remember Him.*

Second: *allow the Holy Spirt to examine your heart. If you need to confess sin - do it. If you need accountability - ask for it. If there's a wrong you need to make right – make it right. God will give you strength. Ask for prayer from those in your group.*

third: *take communion! Get some bread and juice. Thank Him for His broken body and the blood that He poured for the sins of the world.*

Close with more worship and prayer!

SECTION #4 – DEVOTION TO PRAYER

- *What spoke to you the most in this section?*
- *How important is prayer to you?*
- *Do you have "Tent Time" with Jesus? (share about a place you like to connect with the Lord)*

- *How has prayer aligned you with your heavenly assignment?*
- *Share testimonies of answered prayers...*
- *Pray for specific needs in the group...*

ABOUT THE AUTHOR

Travis Habbershon is a preacher whose passion is to see people walk in the freedom that Jesus paid for on the cross. Once bound by drugs, but now soaring on wings like an eagle and shining the light of Jesus everywhere he goes. He and his wife Kelsey, live in Pennsylvania with their son Haven.

Made in the USA
Columbia, SC
17 February 2024

31673552R00074